They called it
Graveyard Girls

Back in 2001 I shot a series of photos for a friend that were intended for use with her music, and just one year later, Graveyard Girls was born.

Ten years later it has grown to become what is now considered one of the earliest independent modeling outlets, and it has even launched into printed media with Stiff Magazine.

I have to say, this was all pure accident. None of this was ever planned to be a long-term thing.

I don't consider myself to be a photographer or an artist. It honestly amazes me that people like what I do. For those that do, I thank you. This is just a hobby for me, and it will continue as long as I enjoy doing it.

This book is a representation of how it started. Some of the models are experienced. Some are not. Some don't even consider themselves to be models. It's just fun for all of us.

The first nine sets featured are new for 2011, and have been purposely shot for this book after I have been absent from shooting for nearly two years. Each one of these girls has demonstrated a lot of interest in what I do, and I am now very happy to have them be part of this book.

The remaining four were part of what was planned to be the final offering of my old website, however I closed the site in 2009 before publishing any of the content to prepare for the launch of StiffMag. I'm glad I finally have the chance to make some of this material available, and the girls have waited for a very long time too.

I hope each of you that has picked up this book find something you like of it. I can't promise there will be another, but I won't say it will never happen.

See you at the graveyard
Shane of the Dead

2011 Series

2009 Series

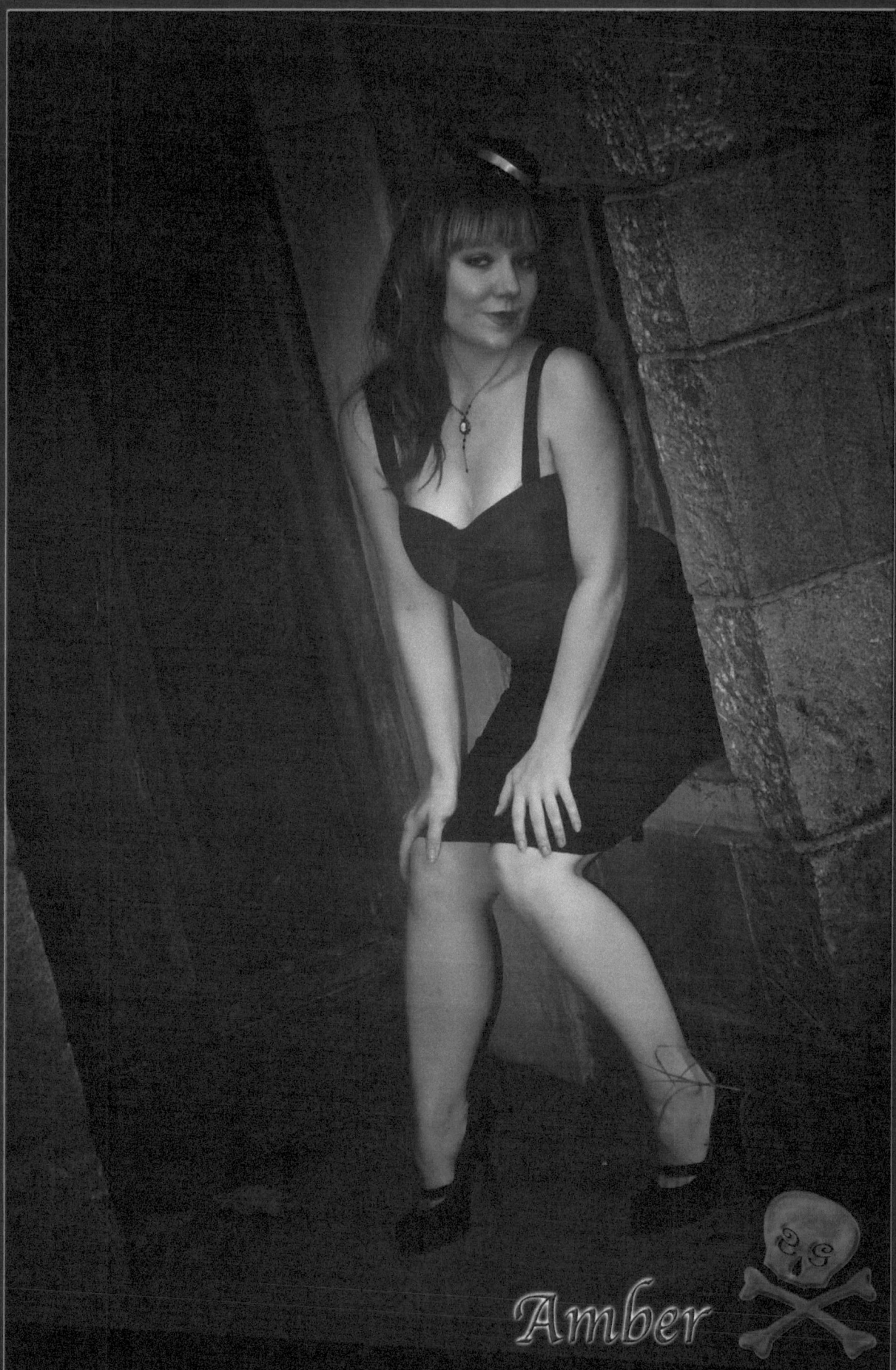

Amber

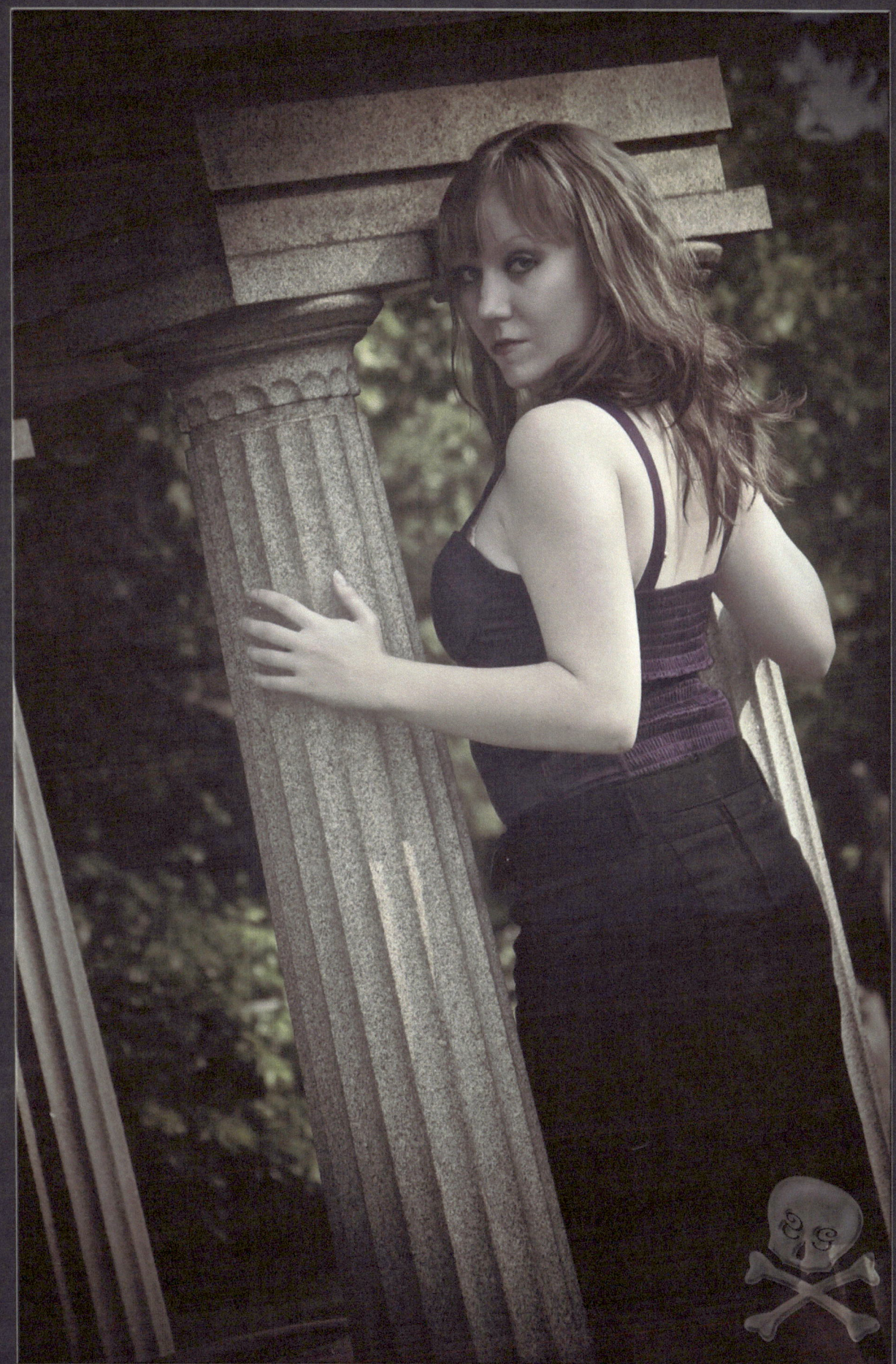

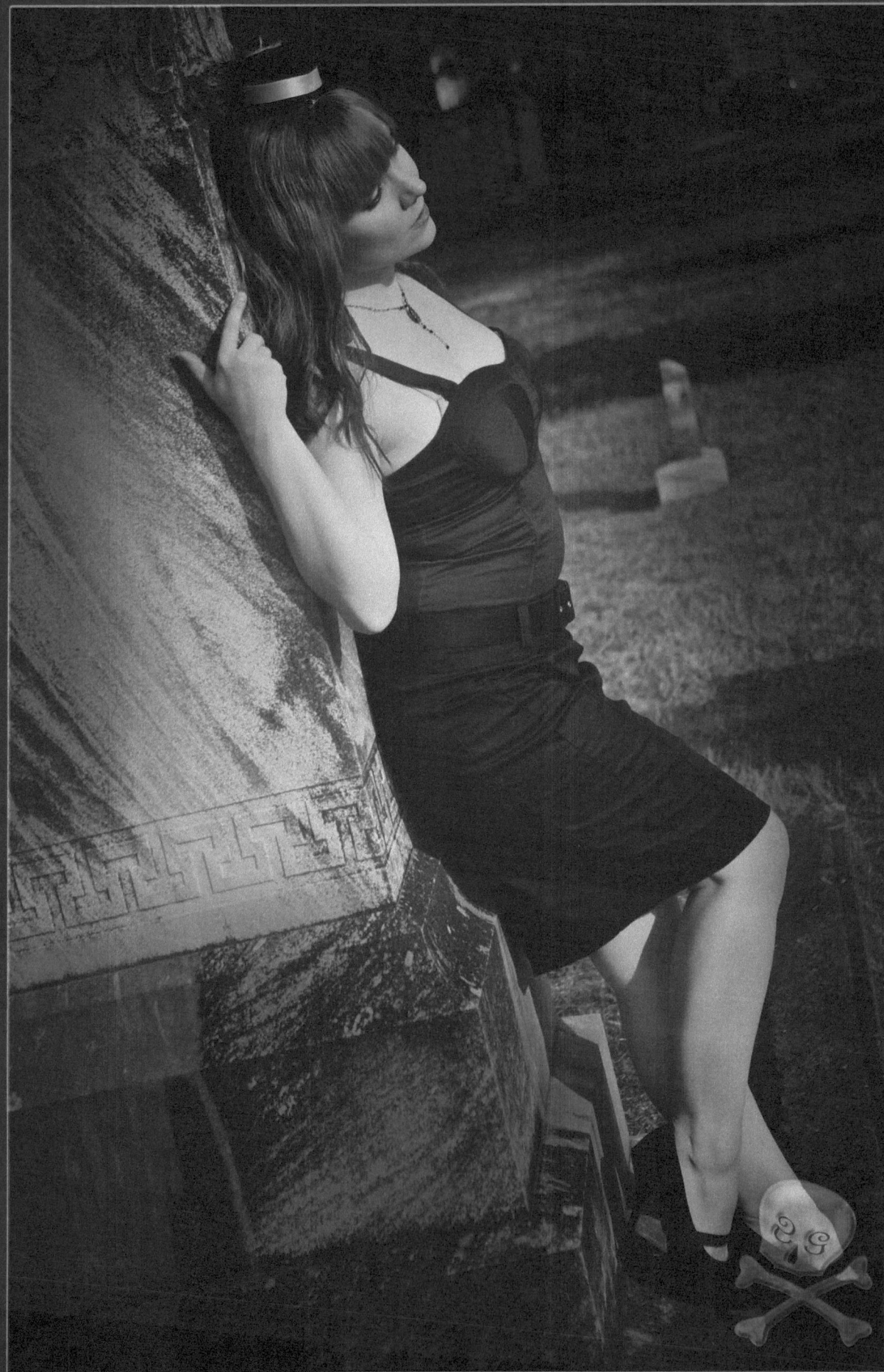

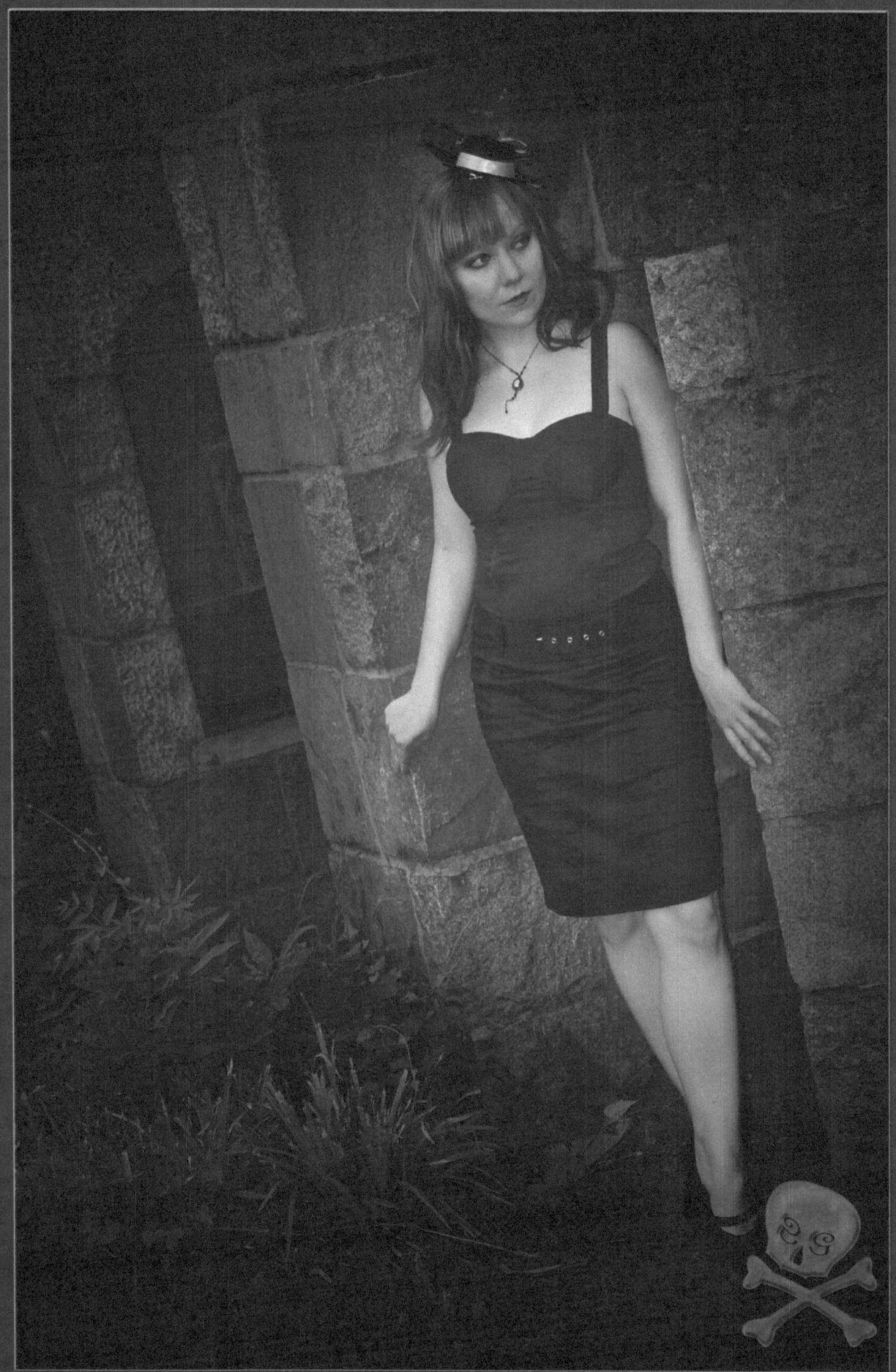

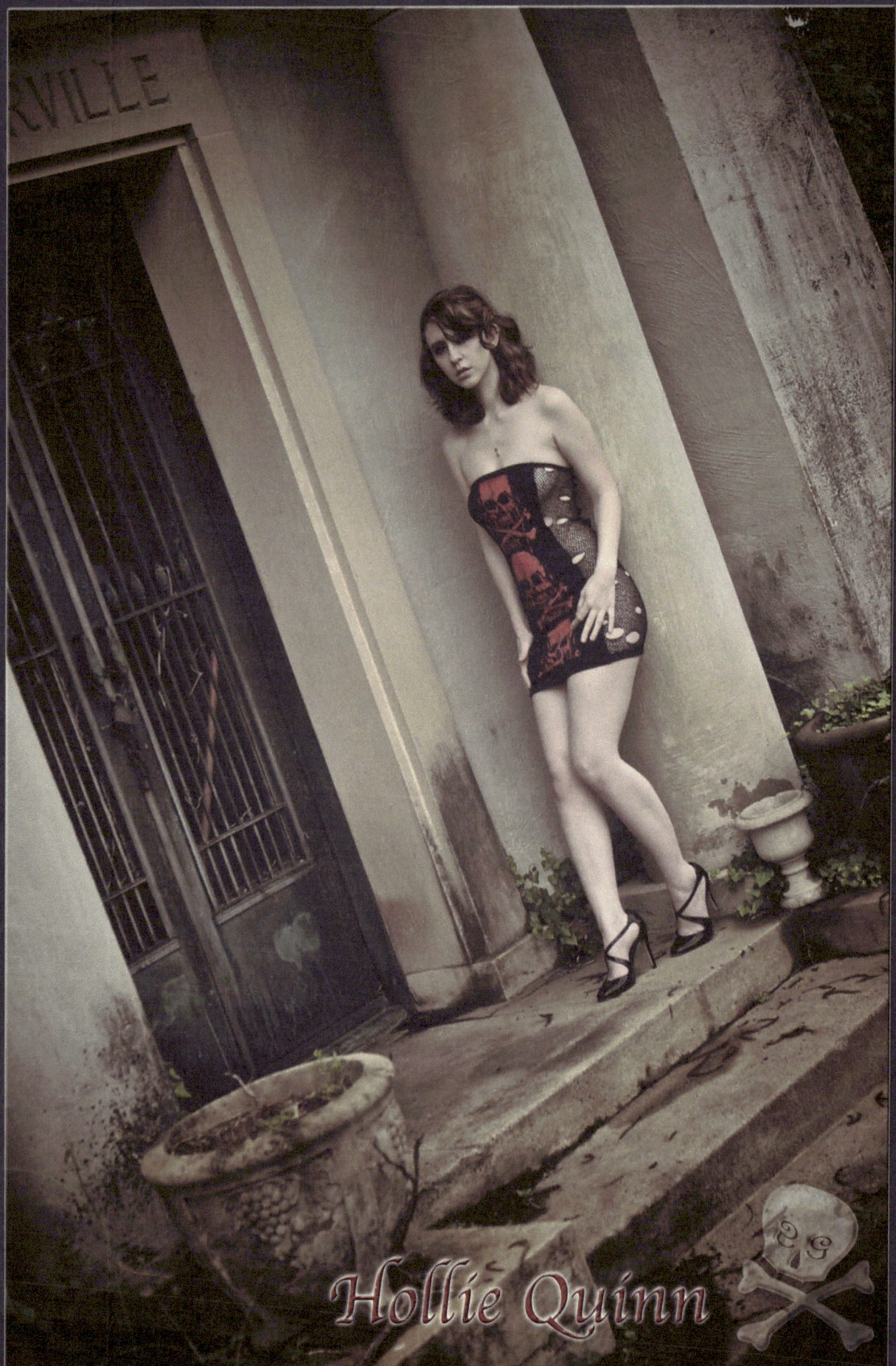

Hollie Quinn

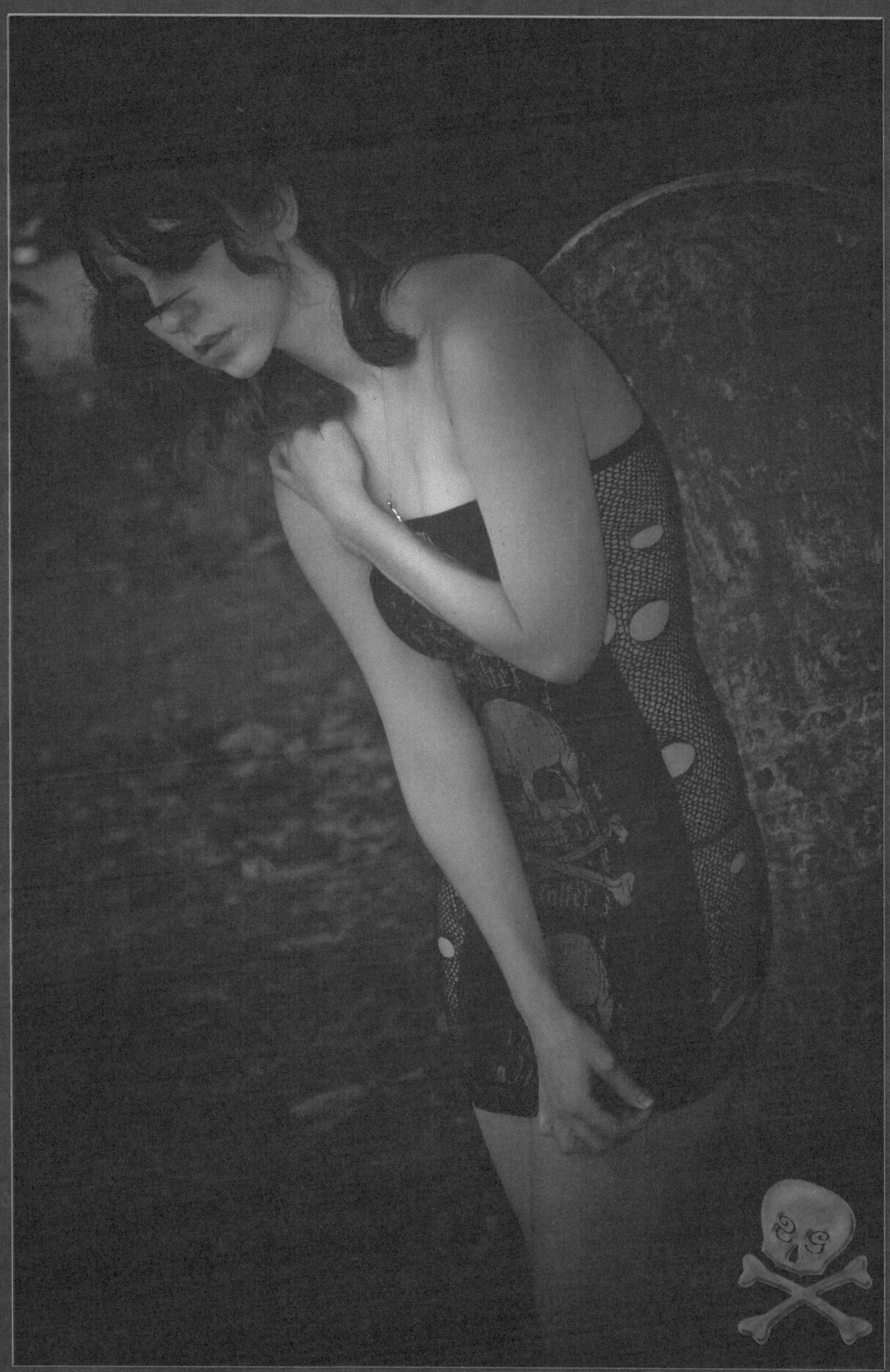

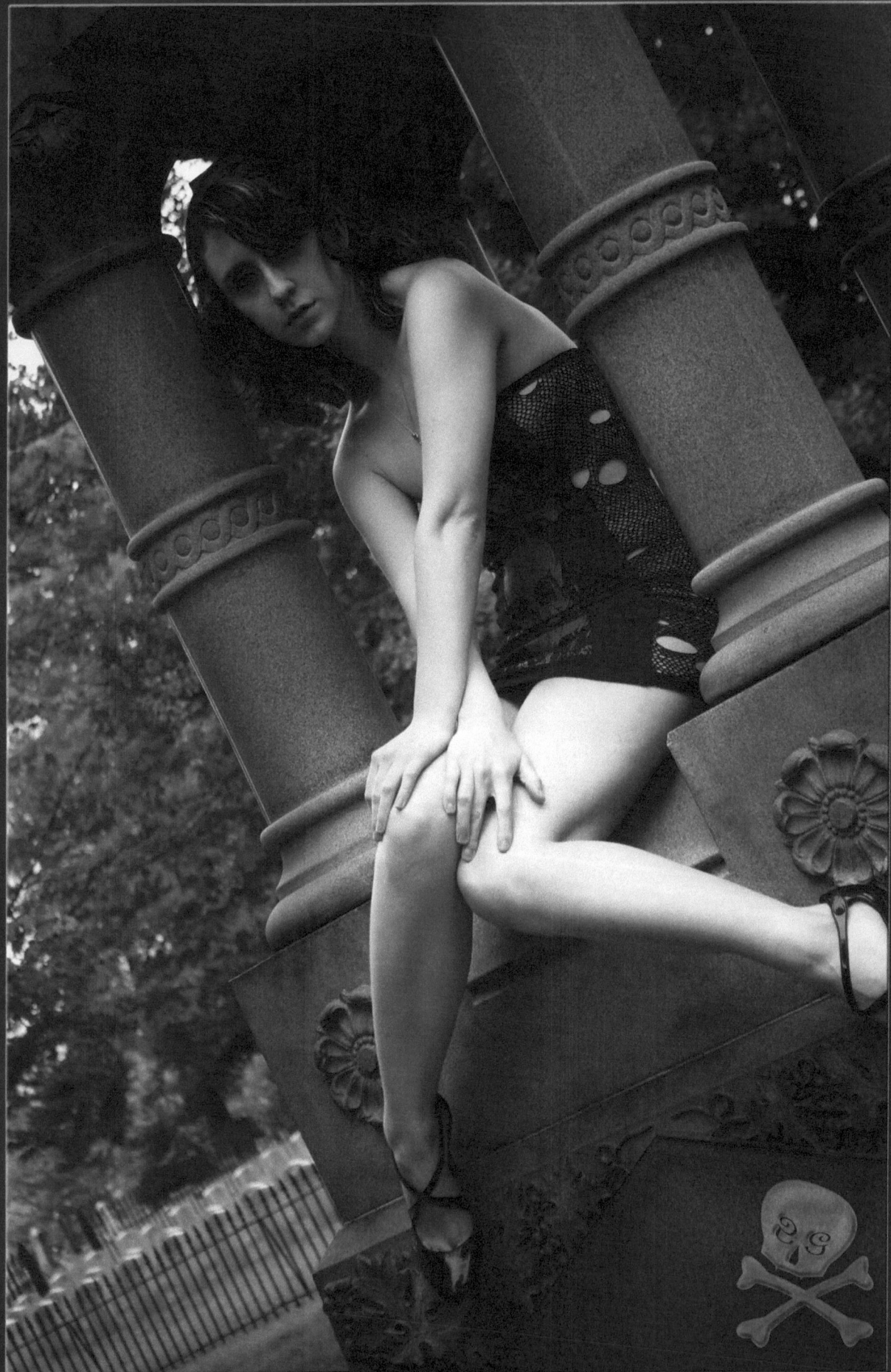

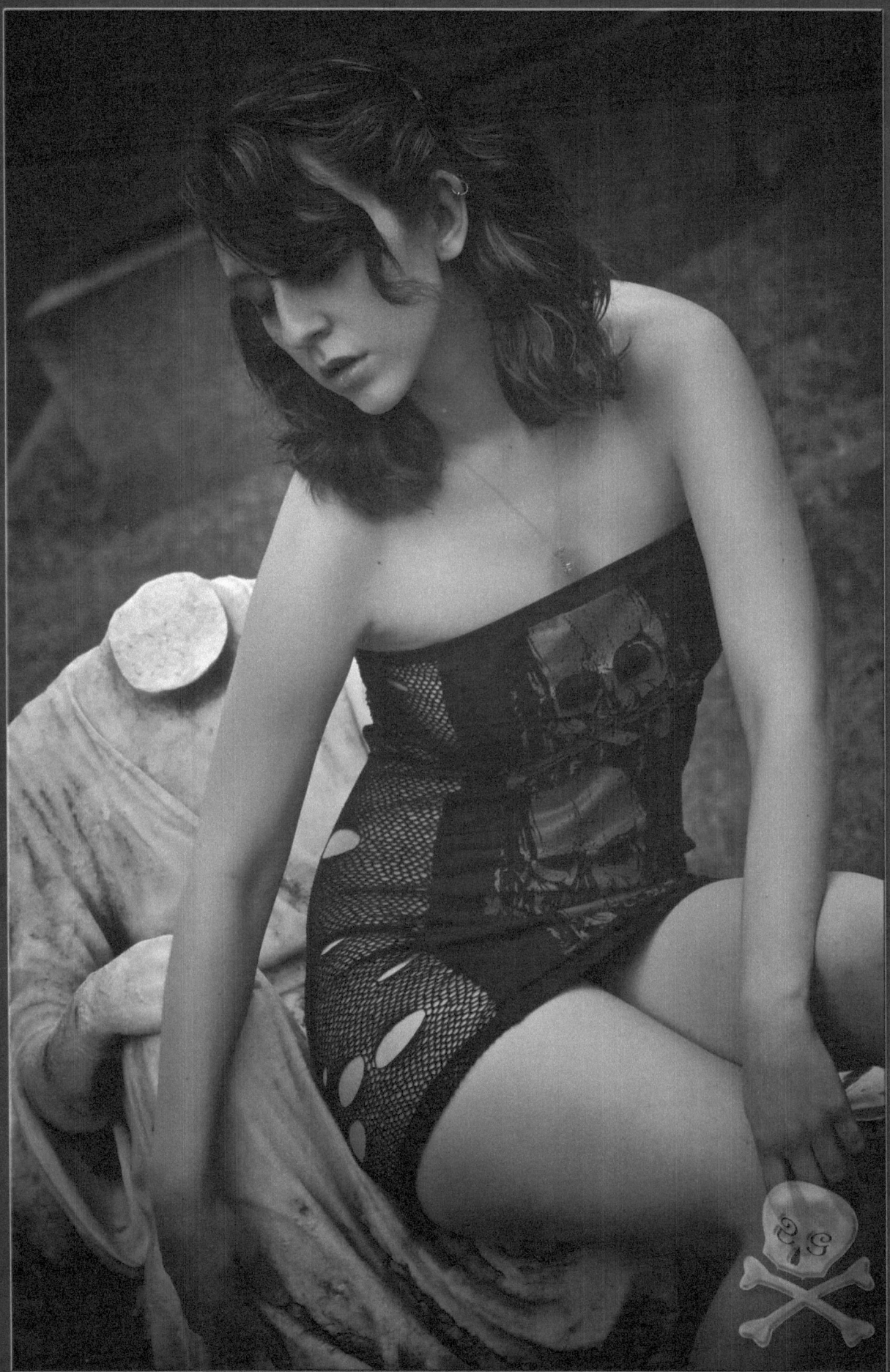

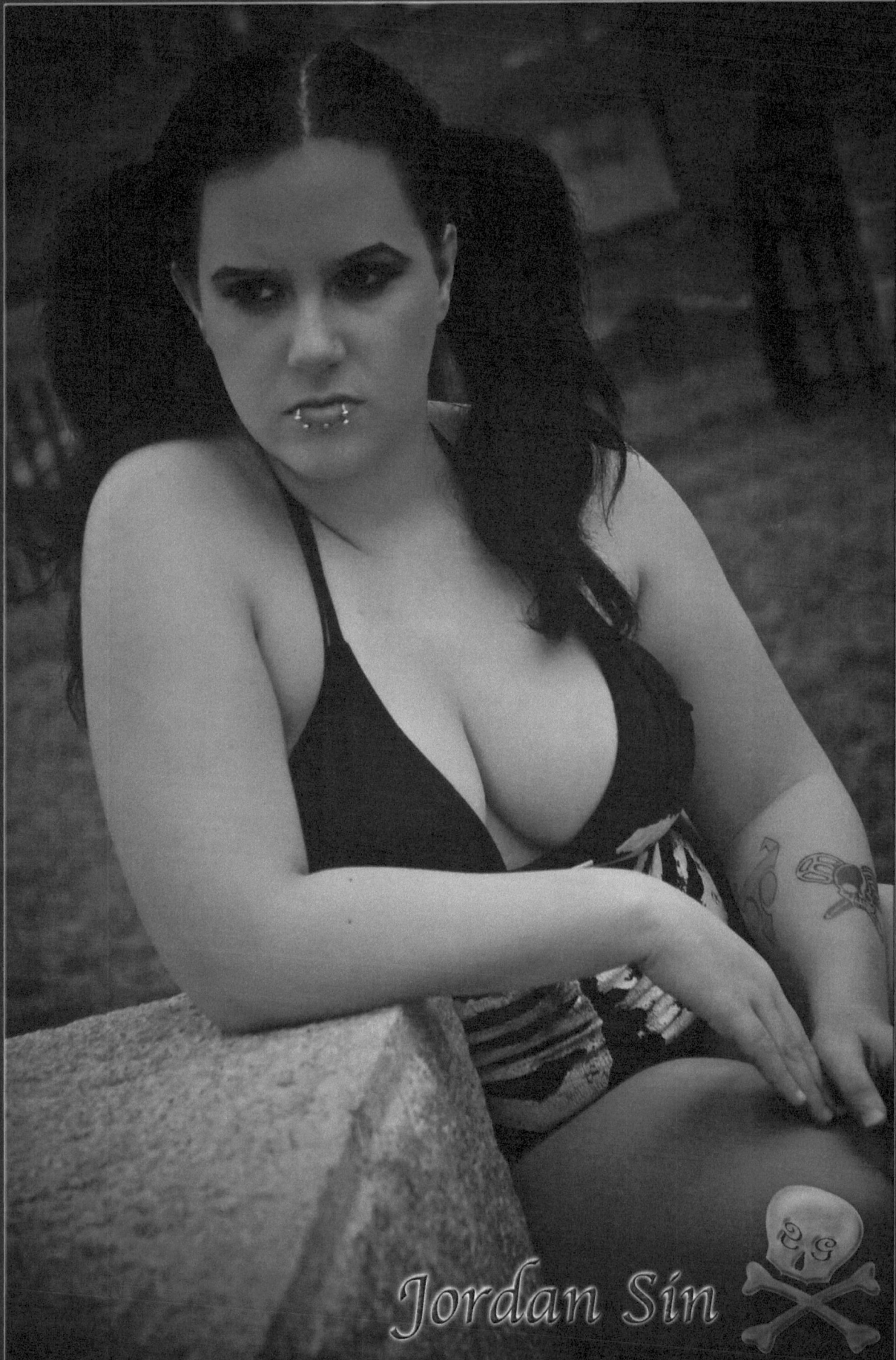

Jordan Sín

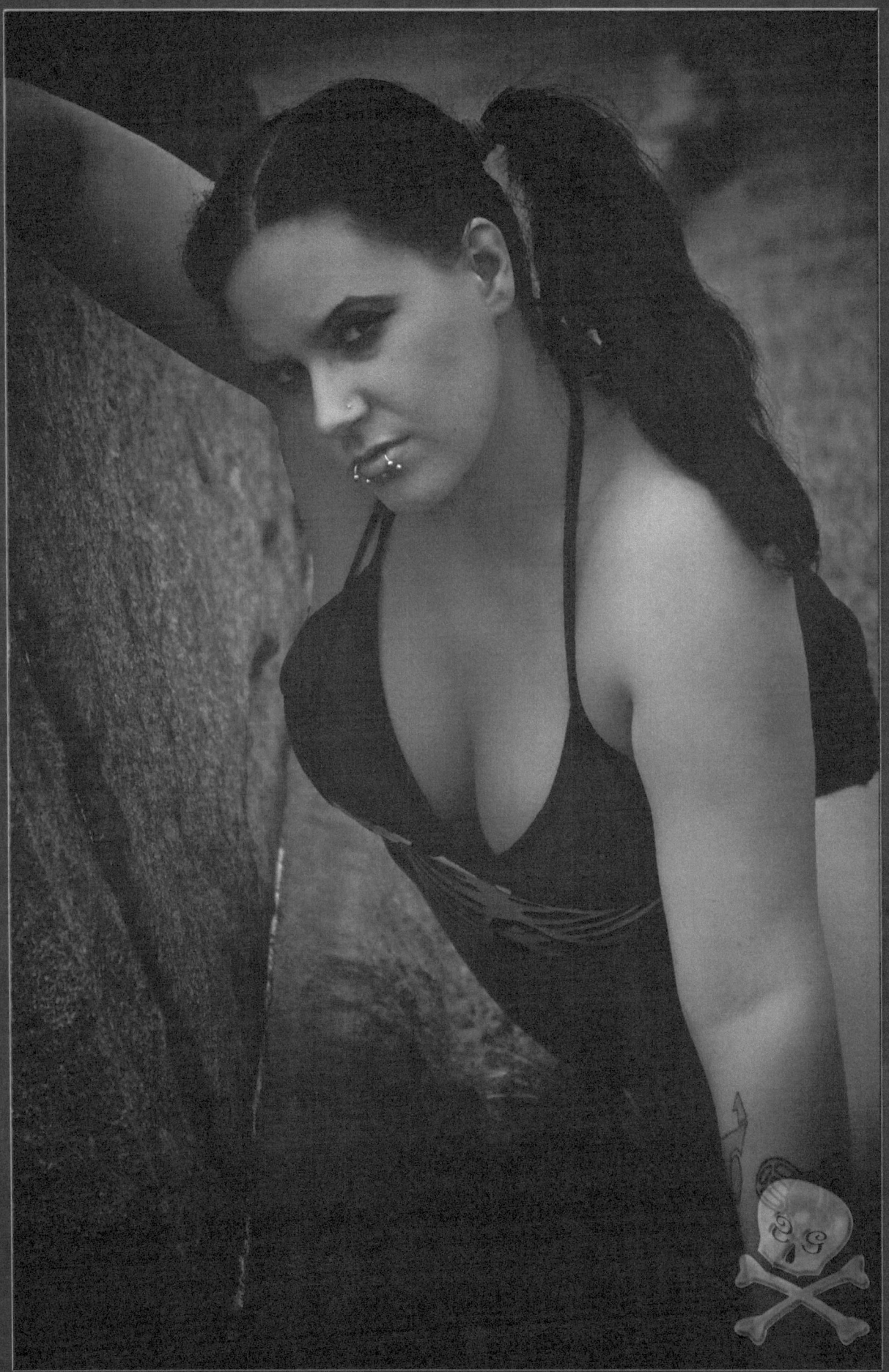

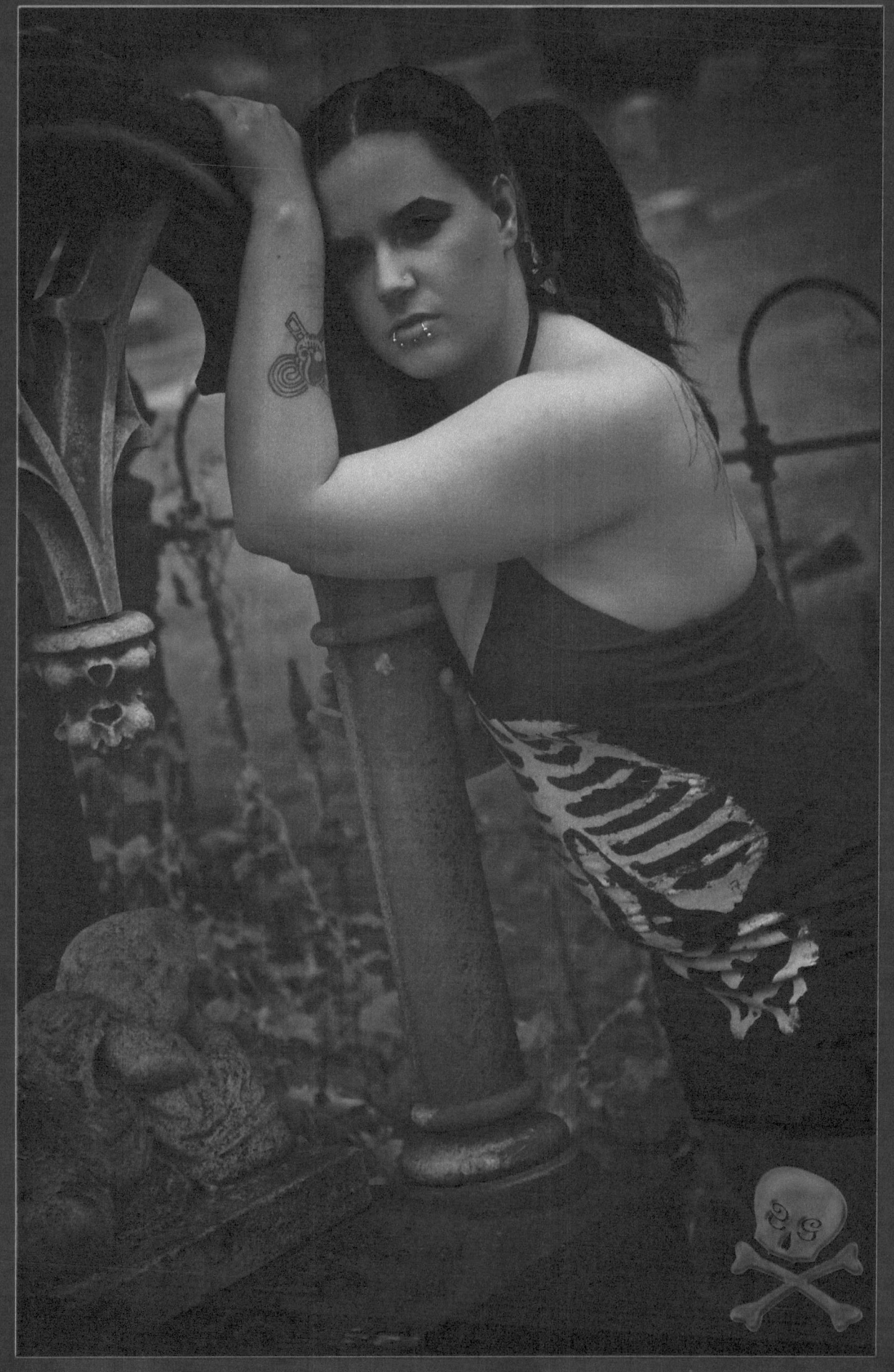

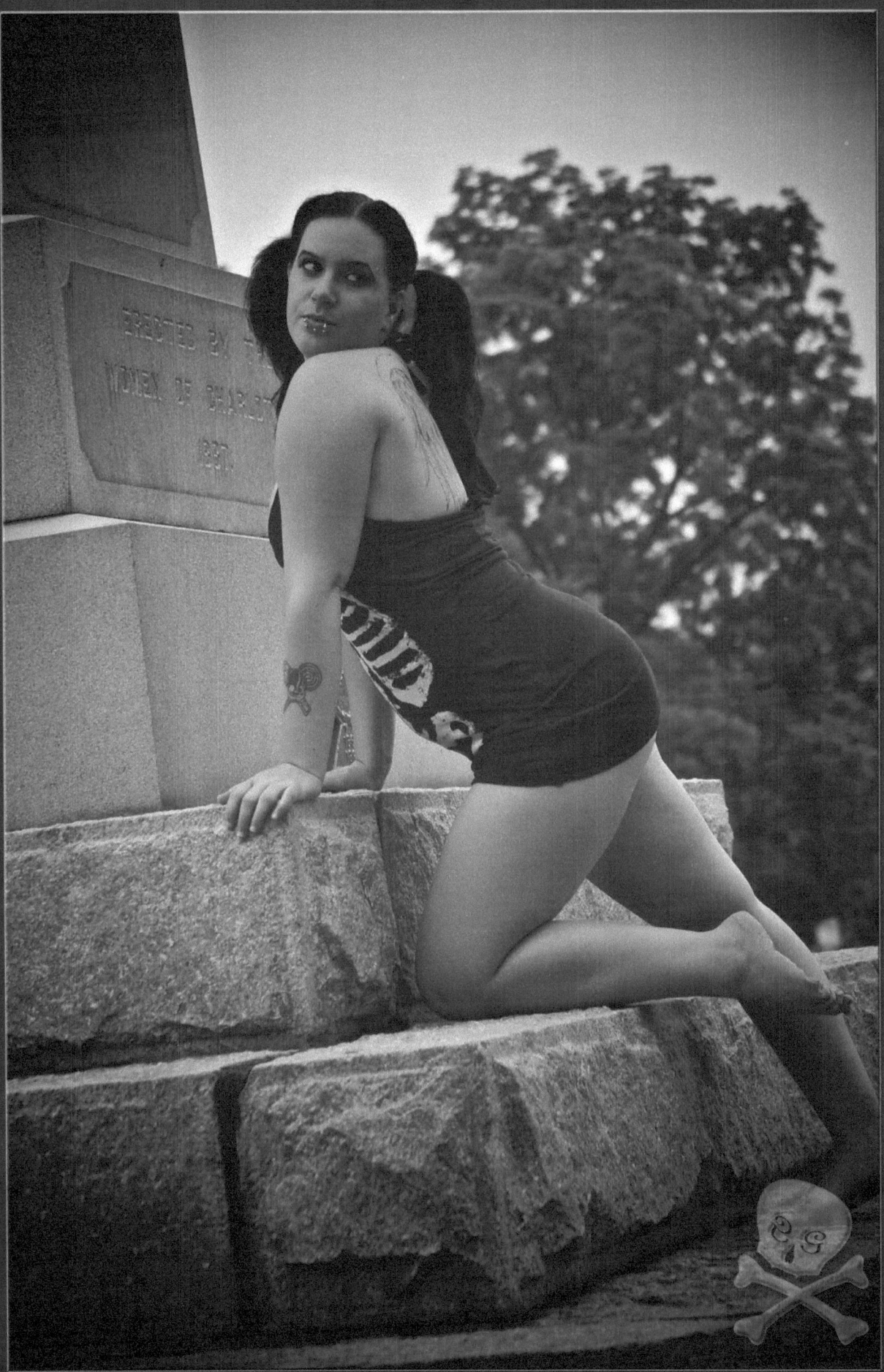

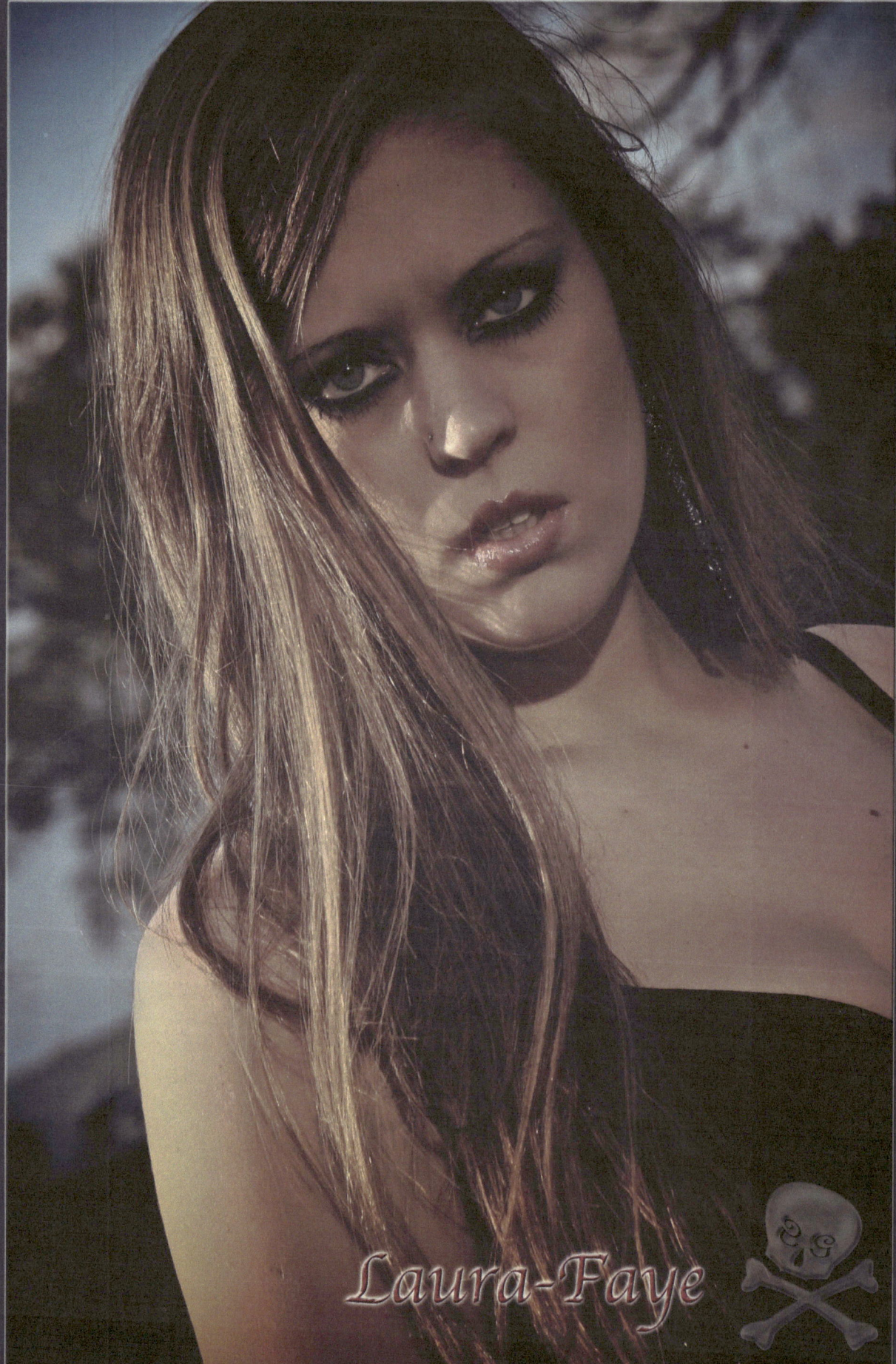

Laura-Faye

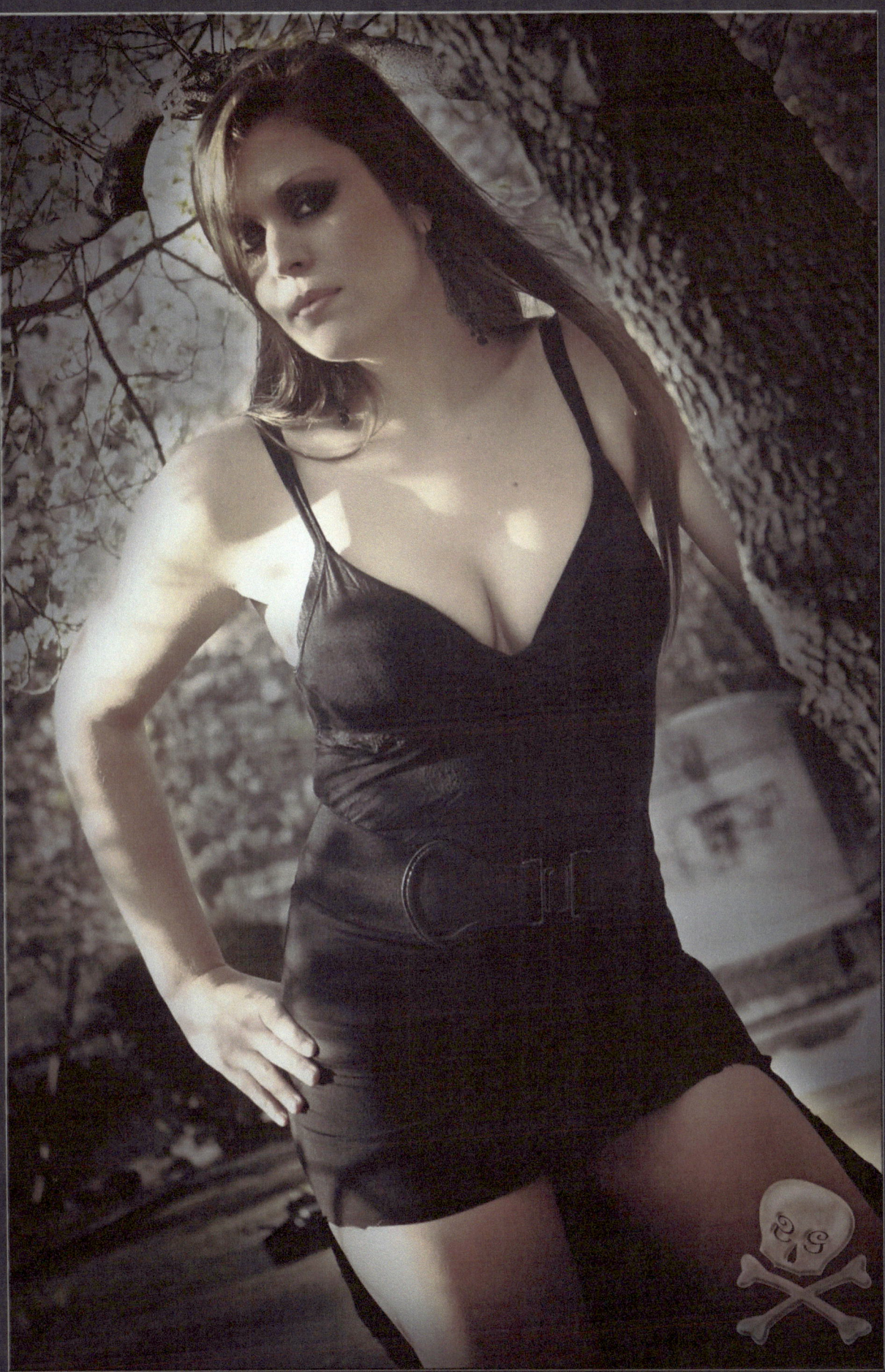

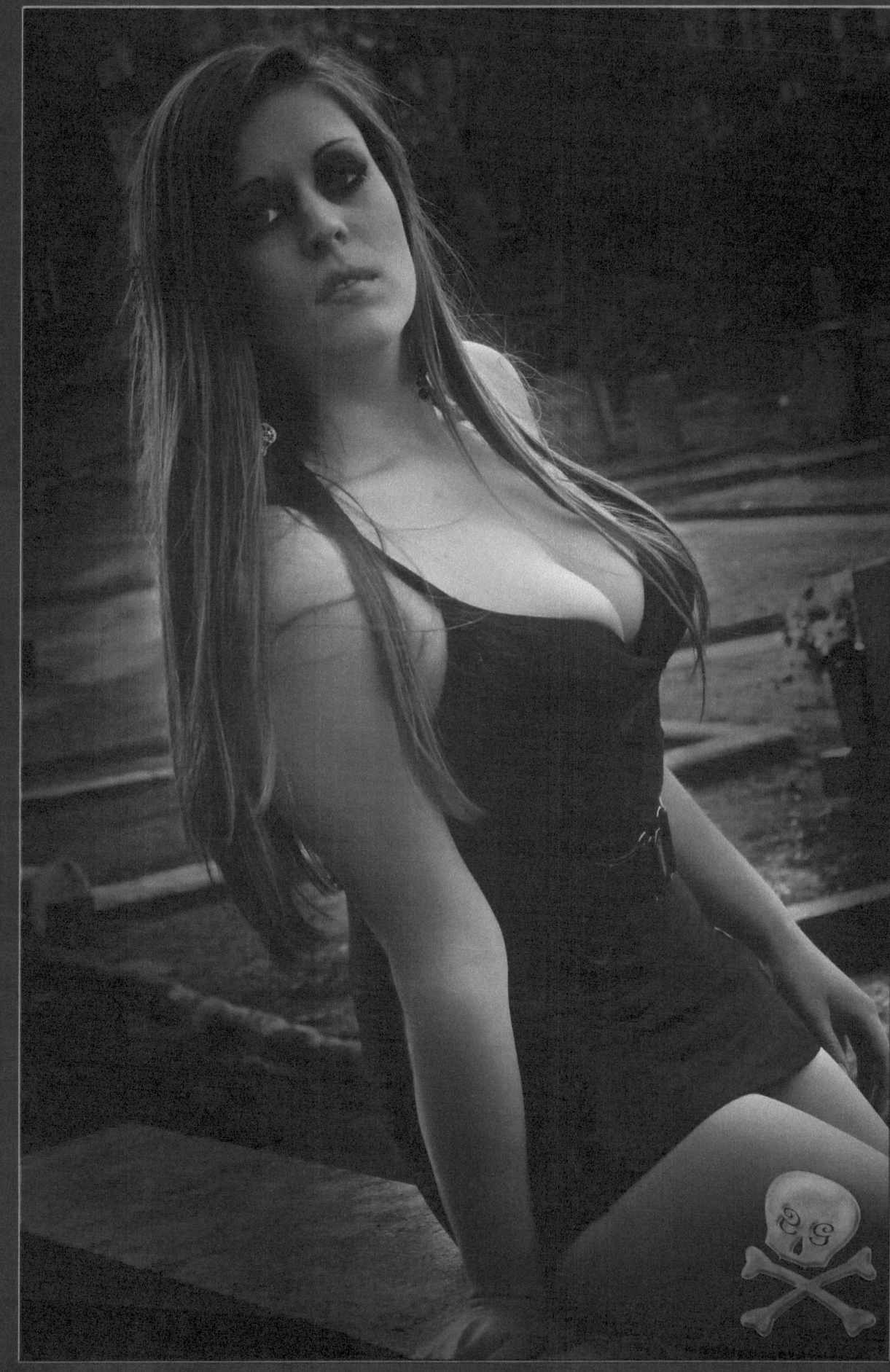

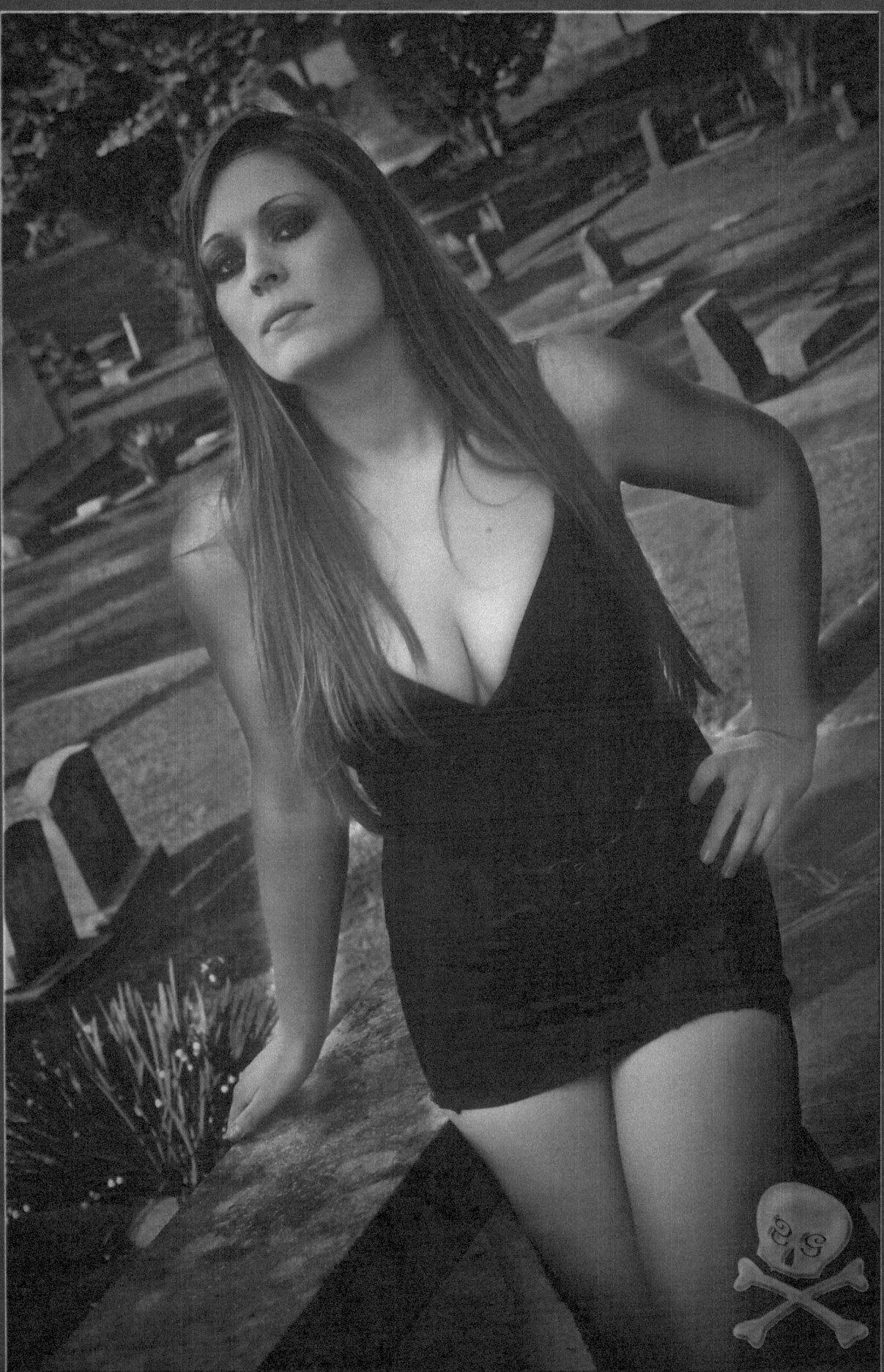

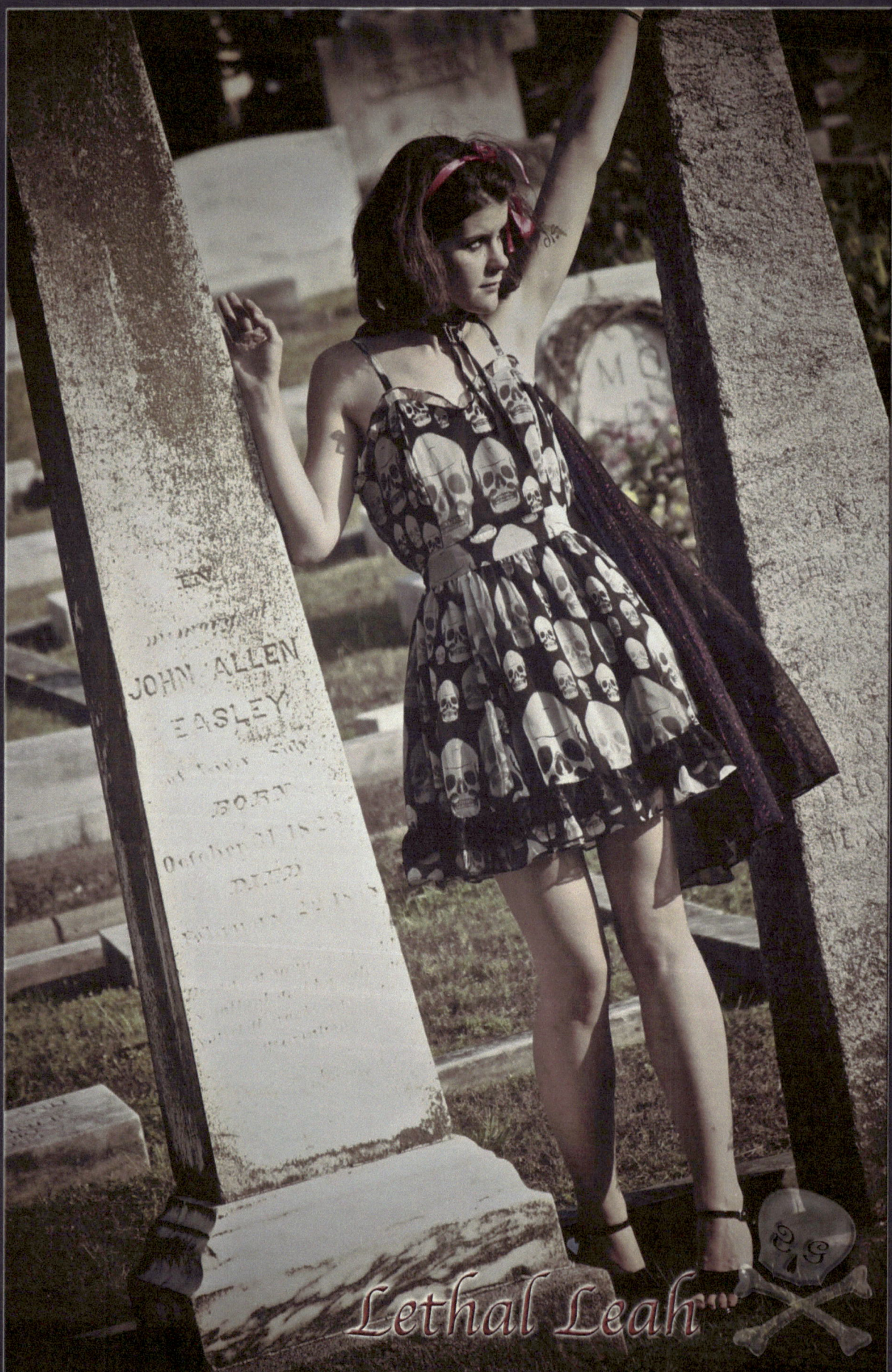

Lethal Leah

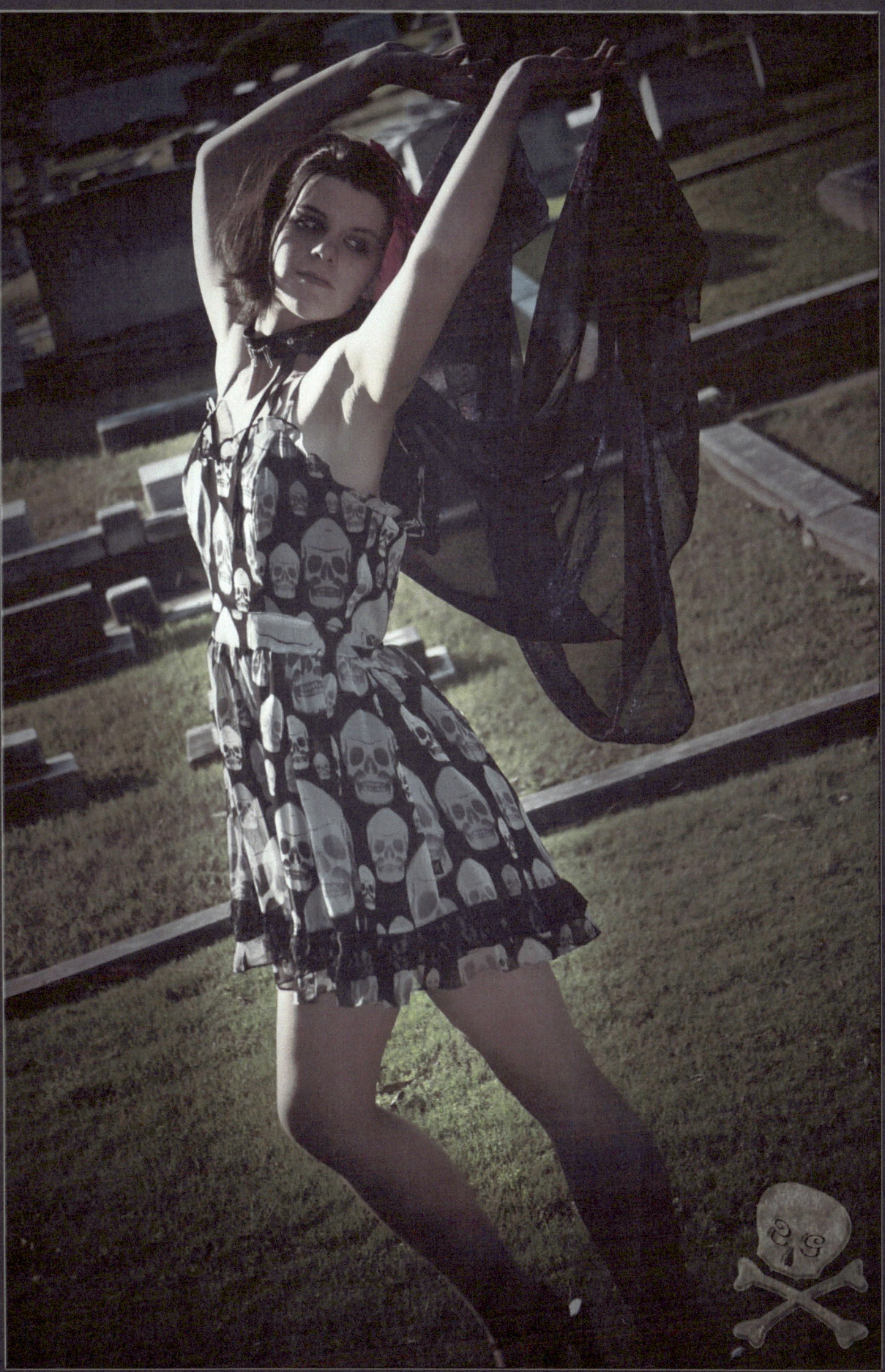

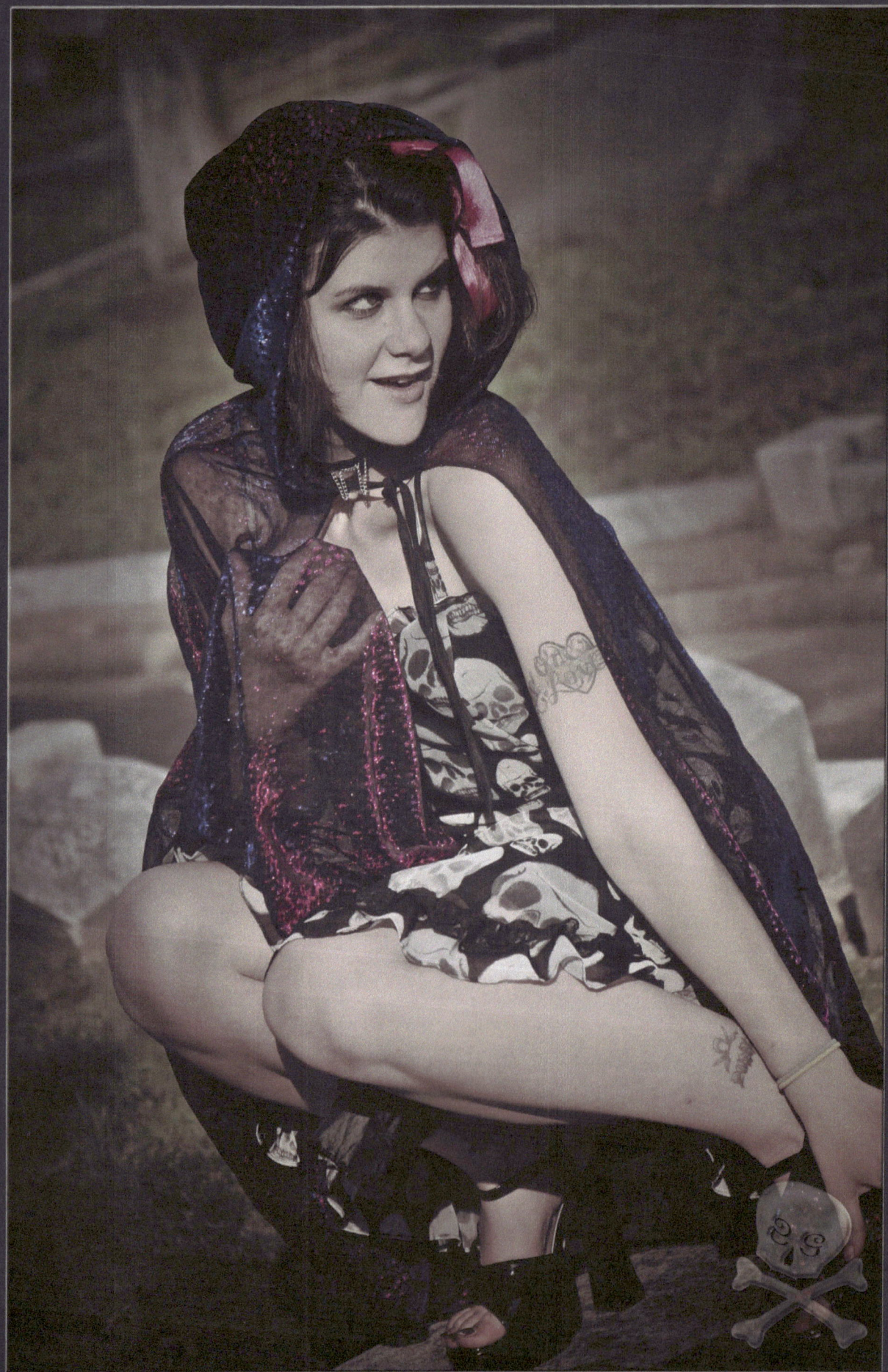

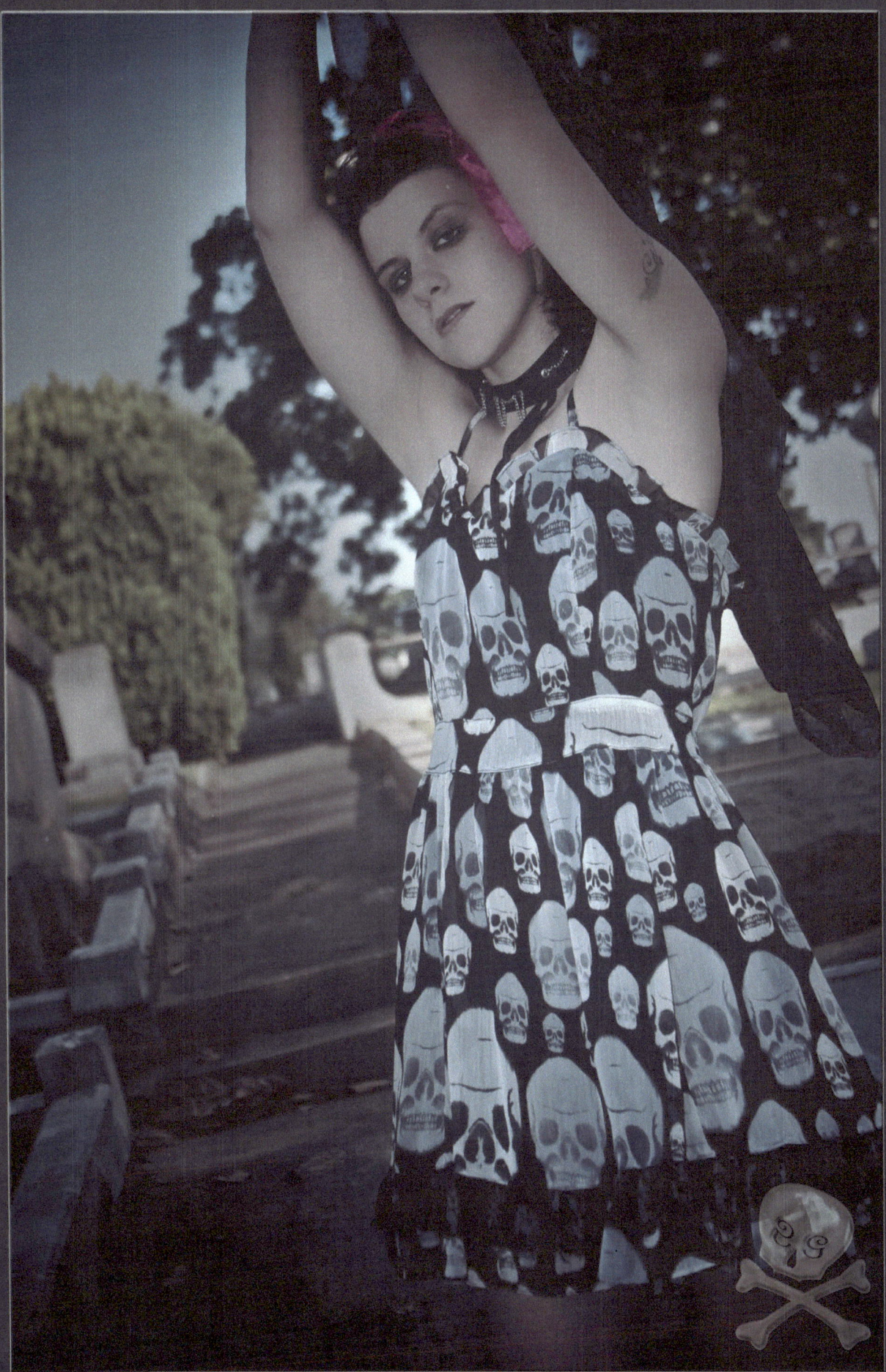

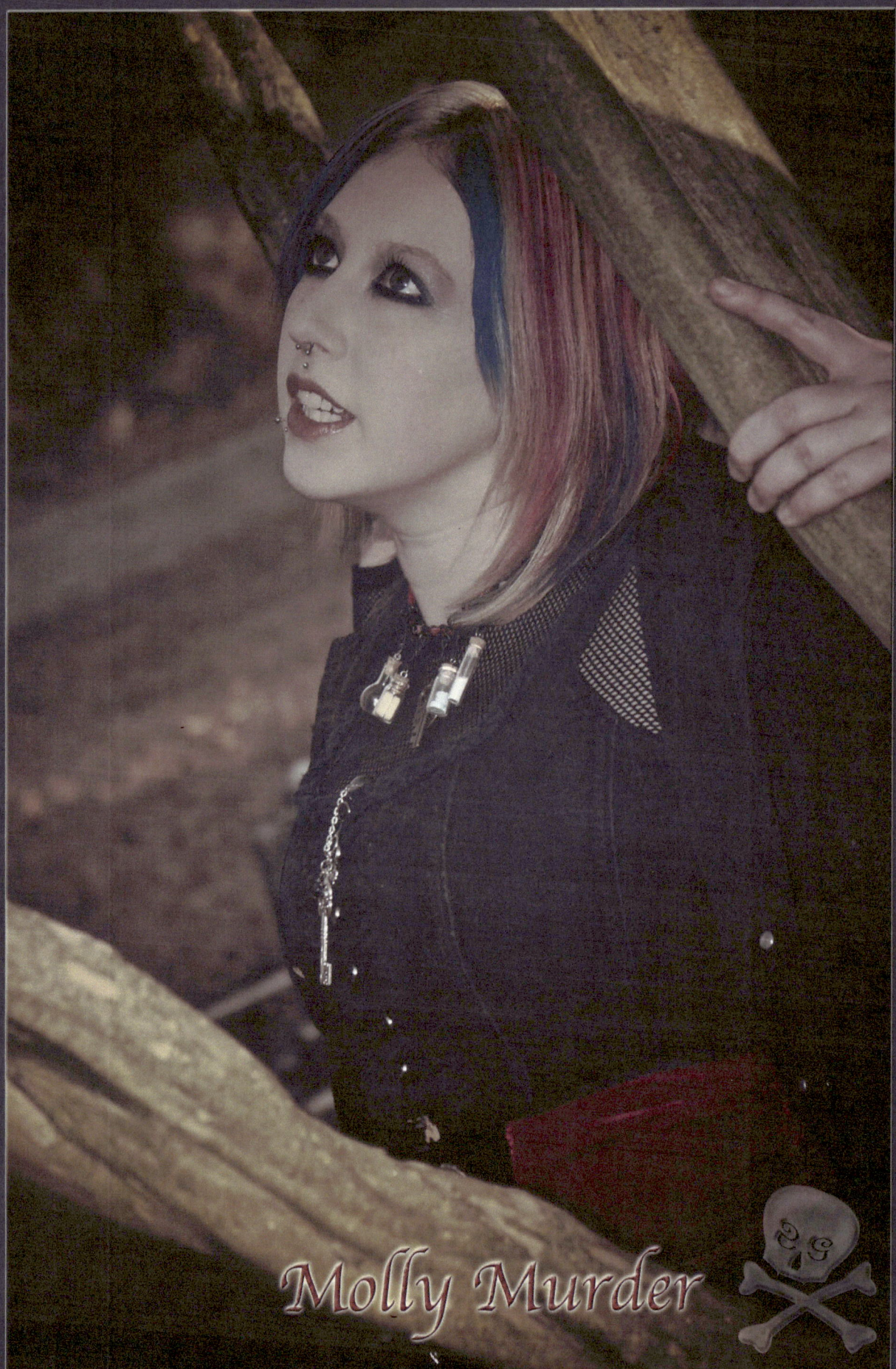

Molly Murder

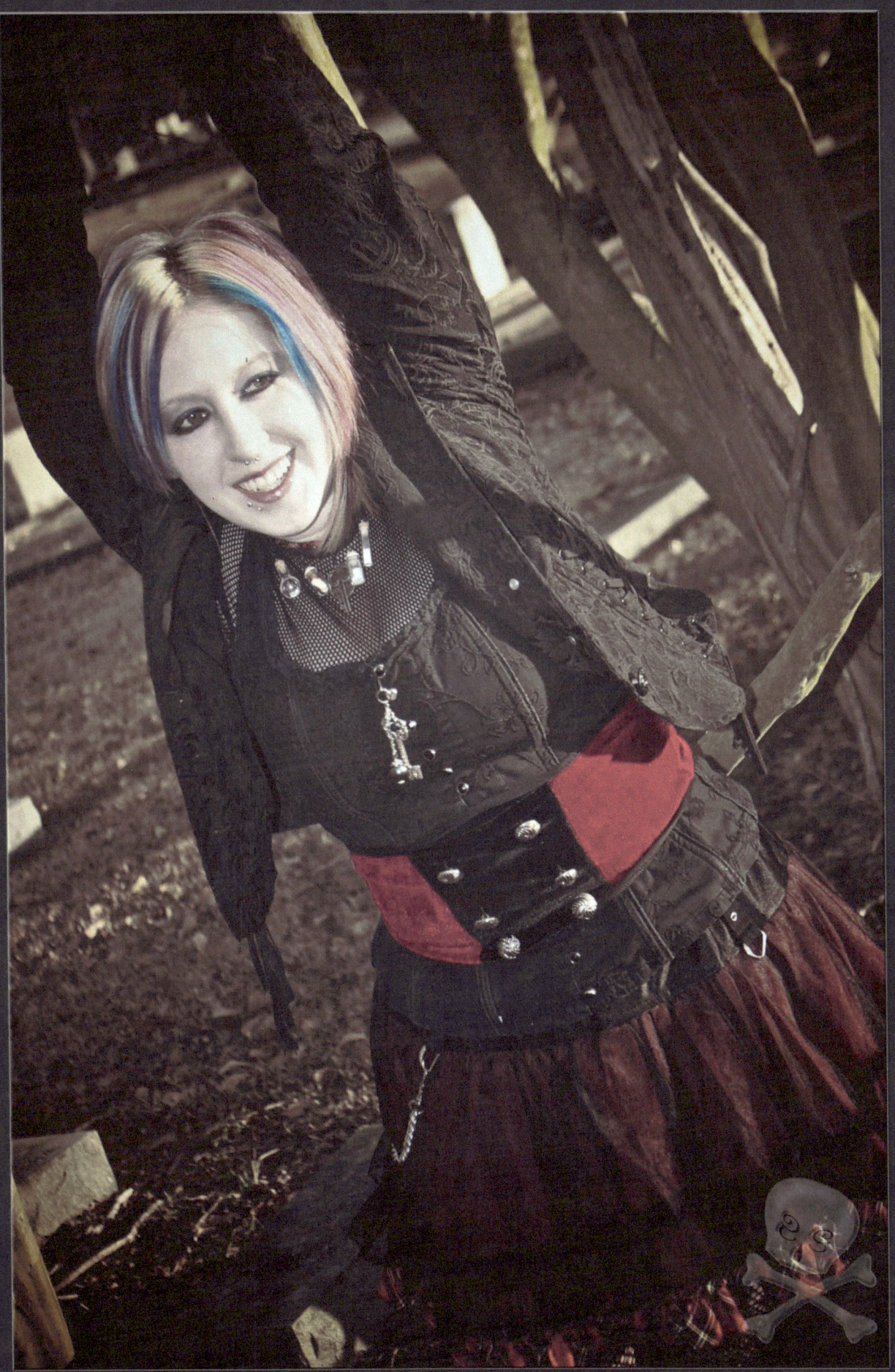

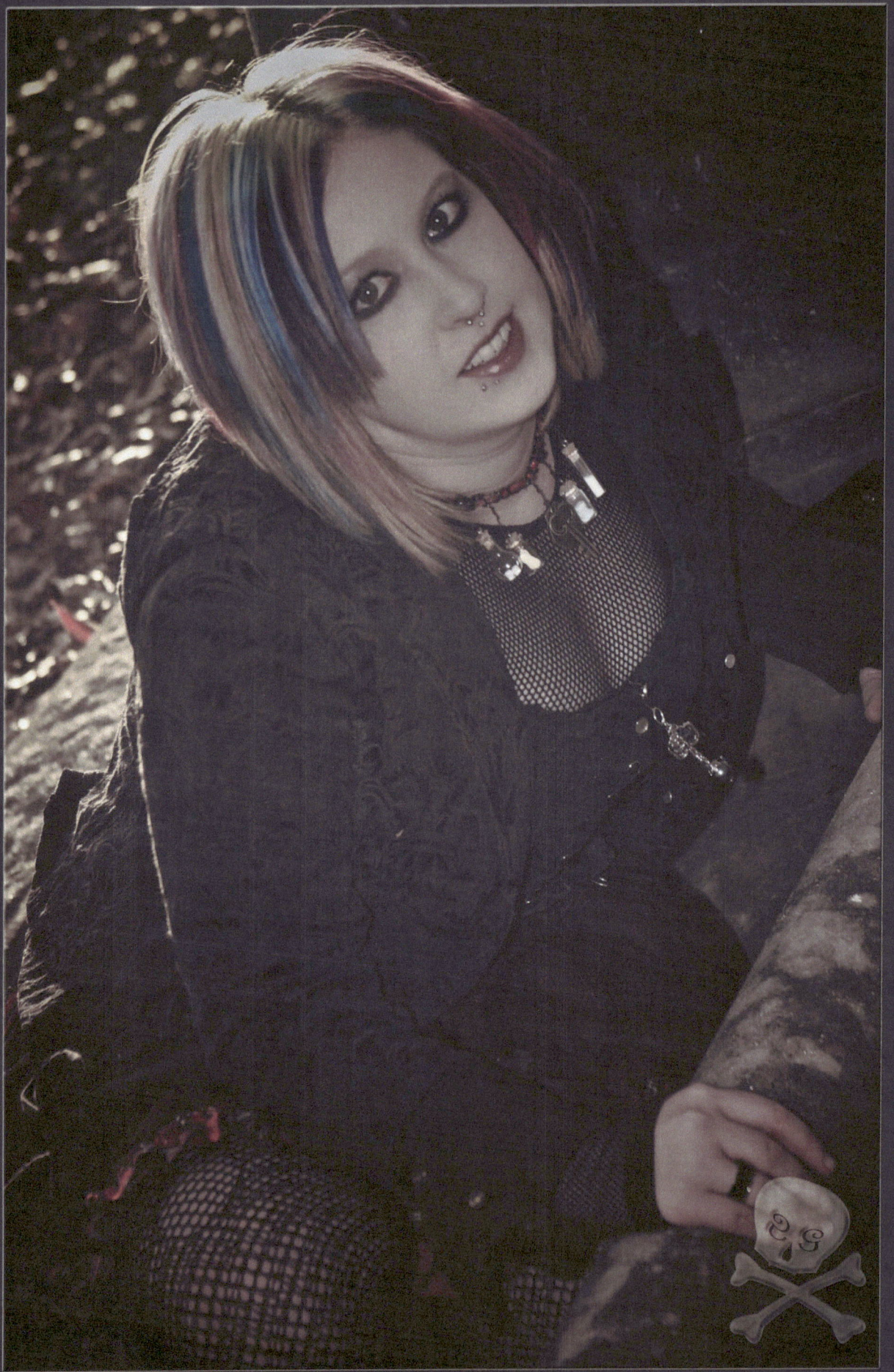

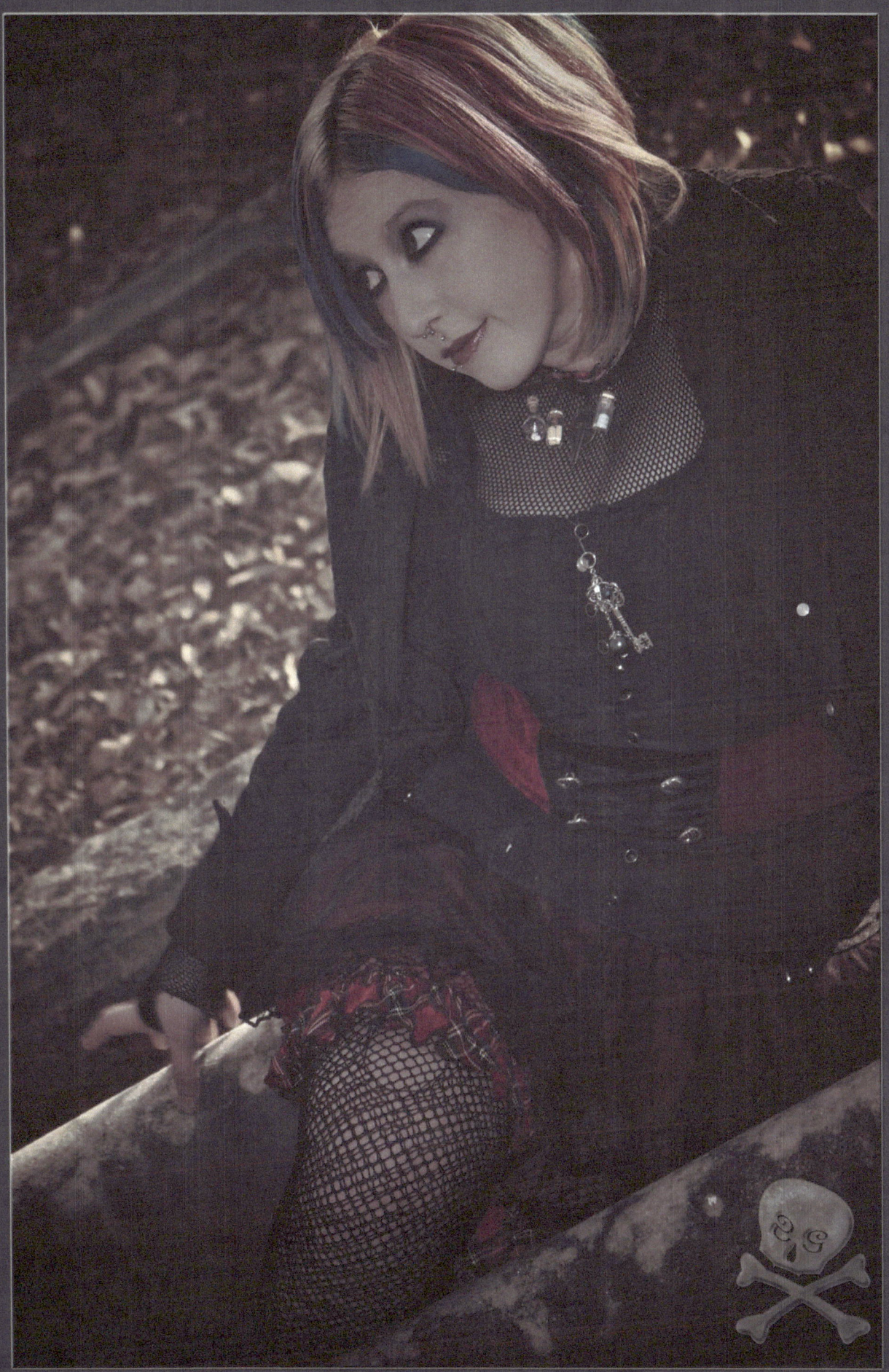

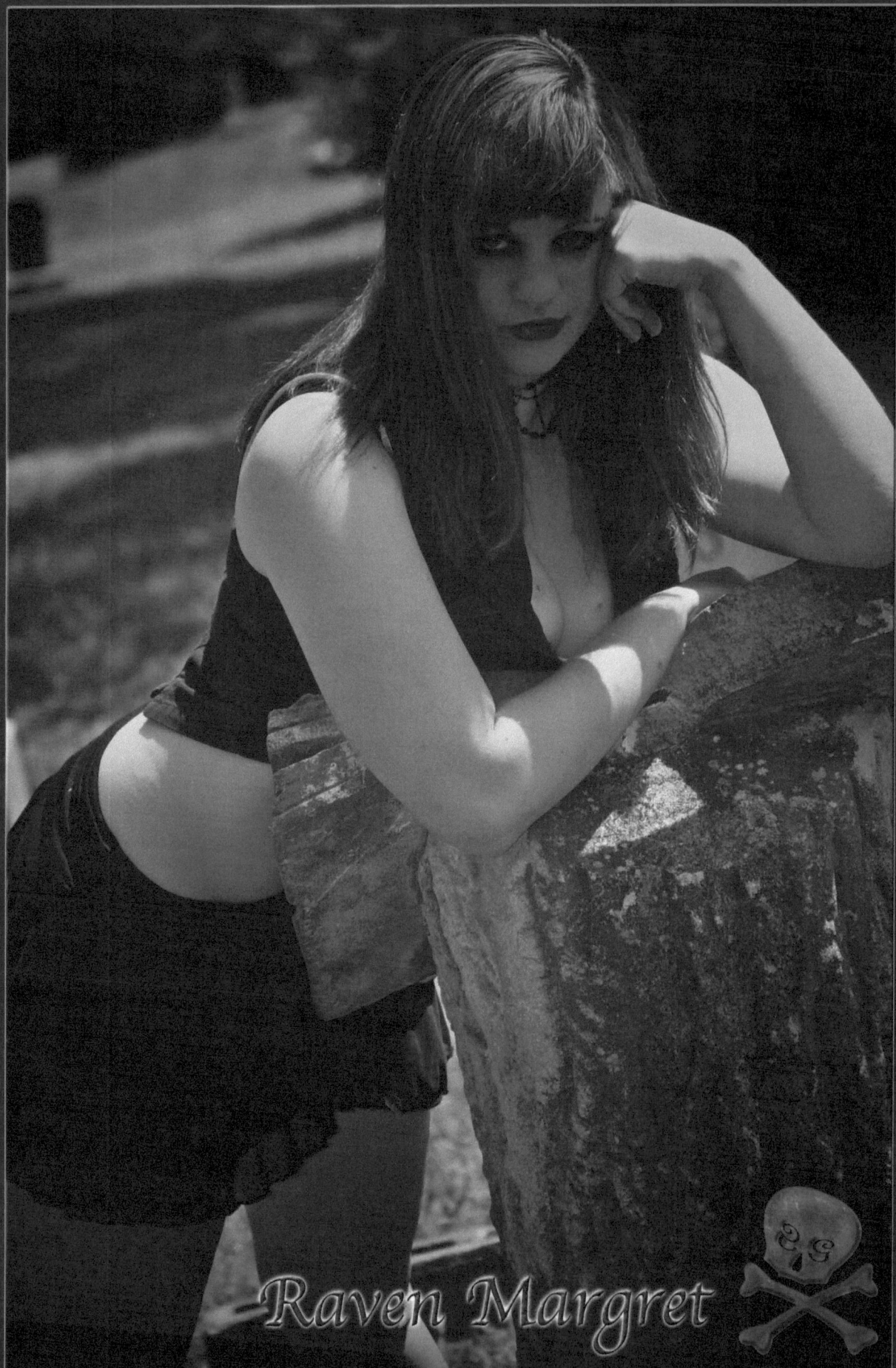

Raven Margret

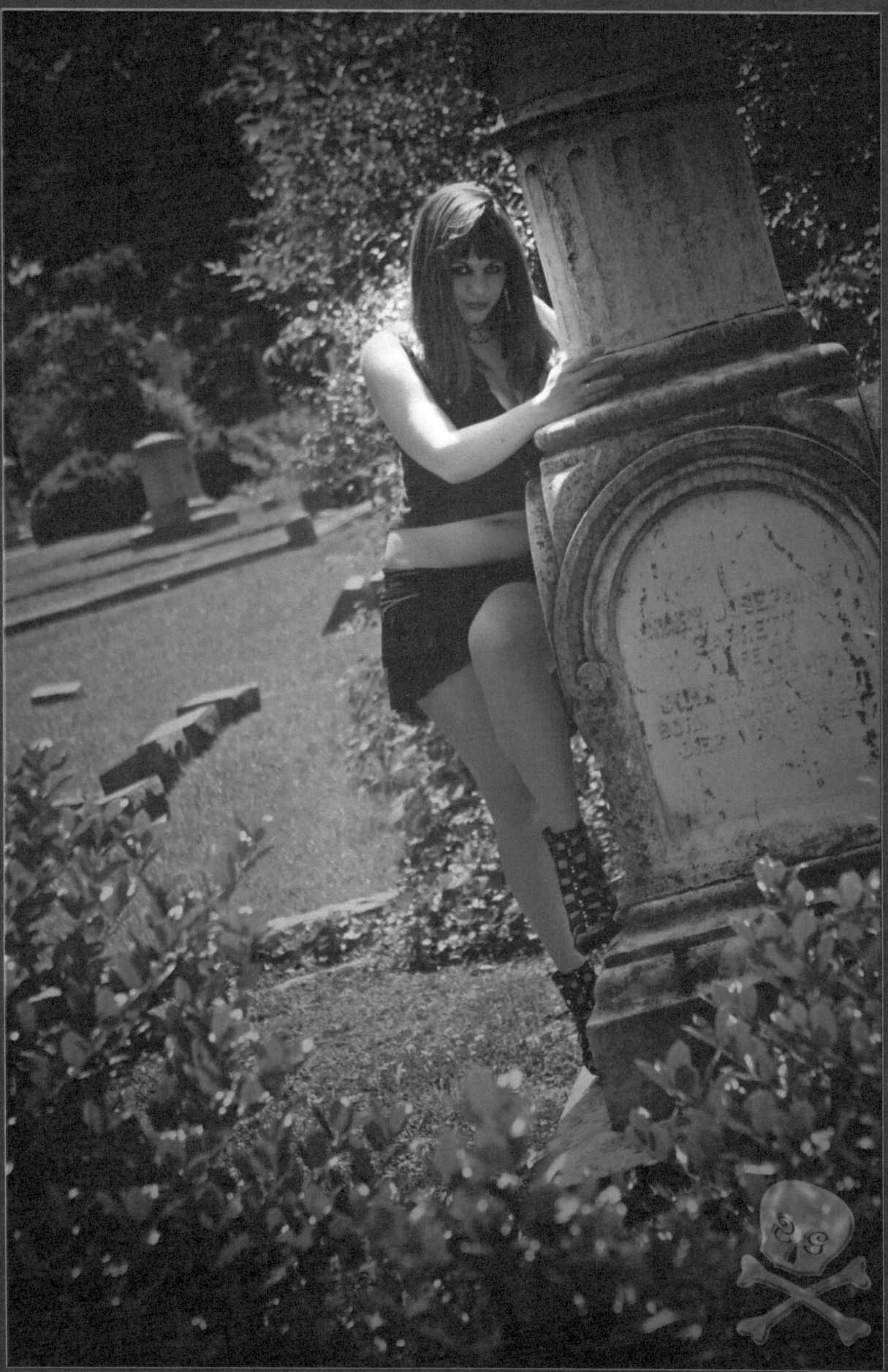

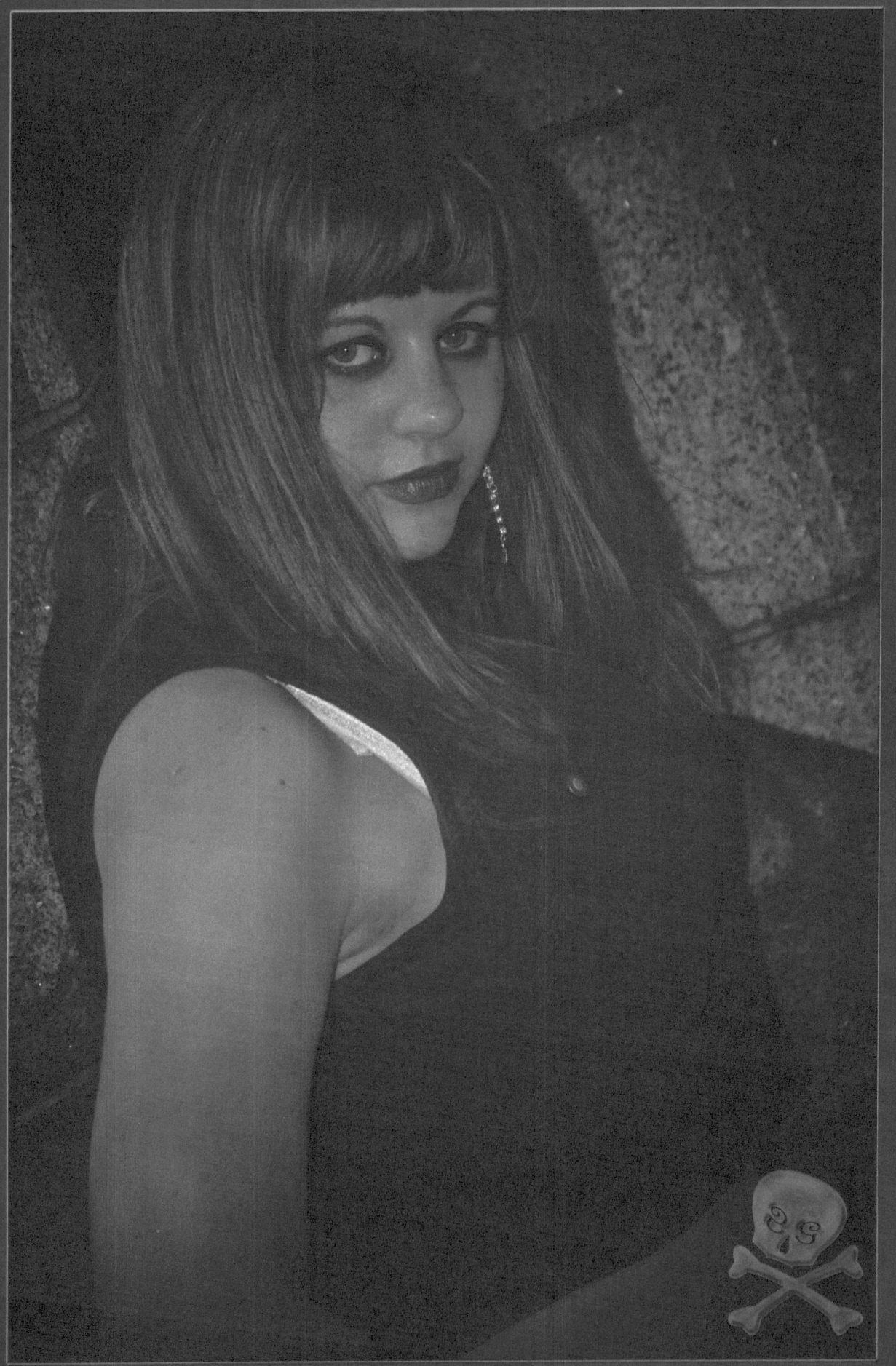

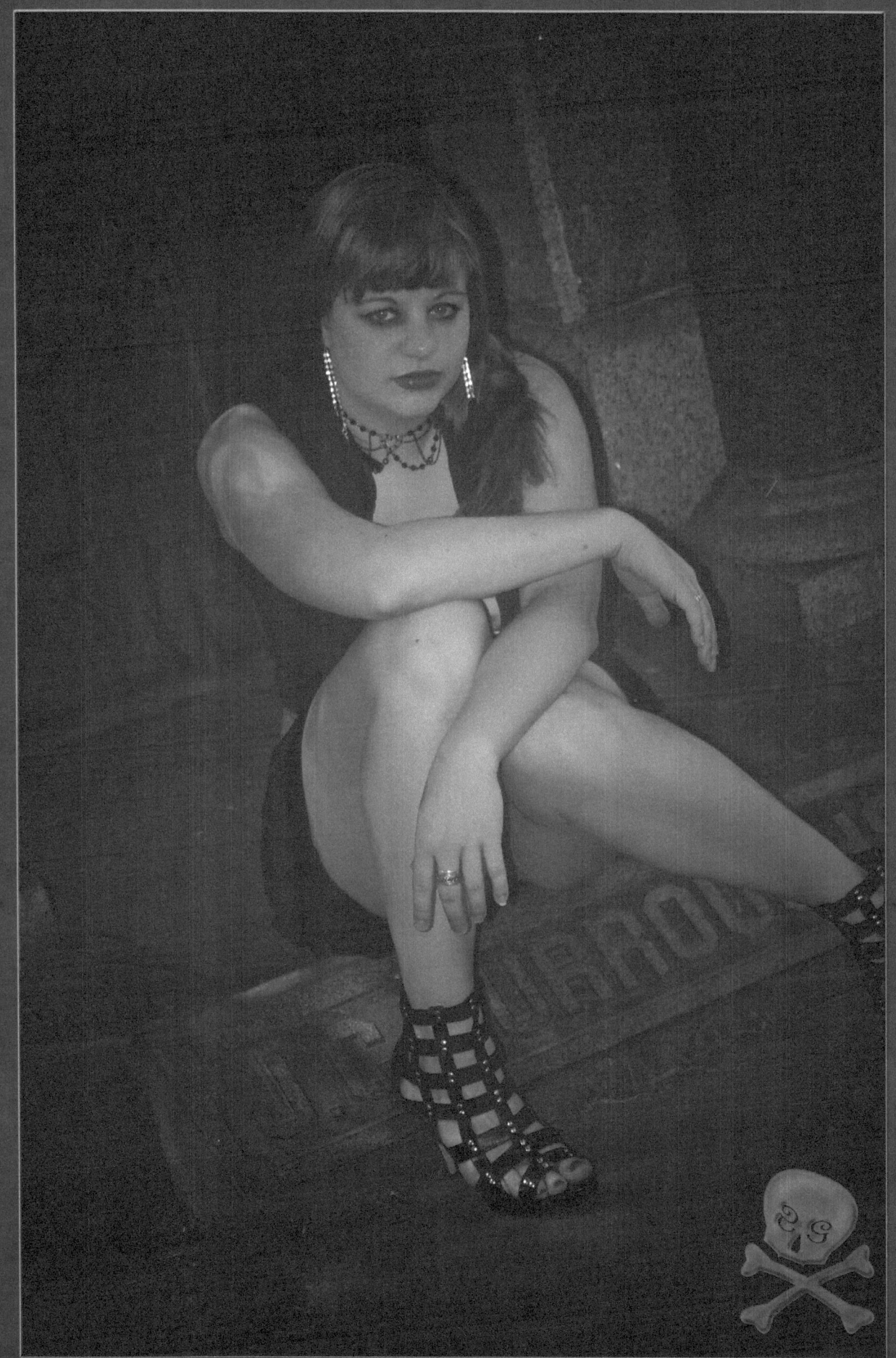

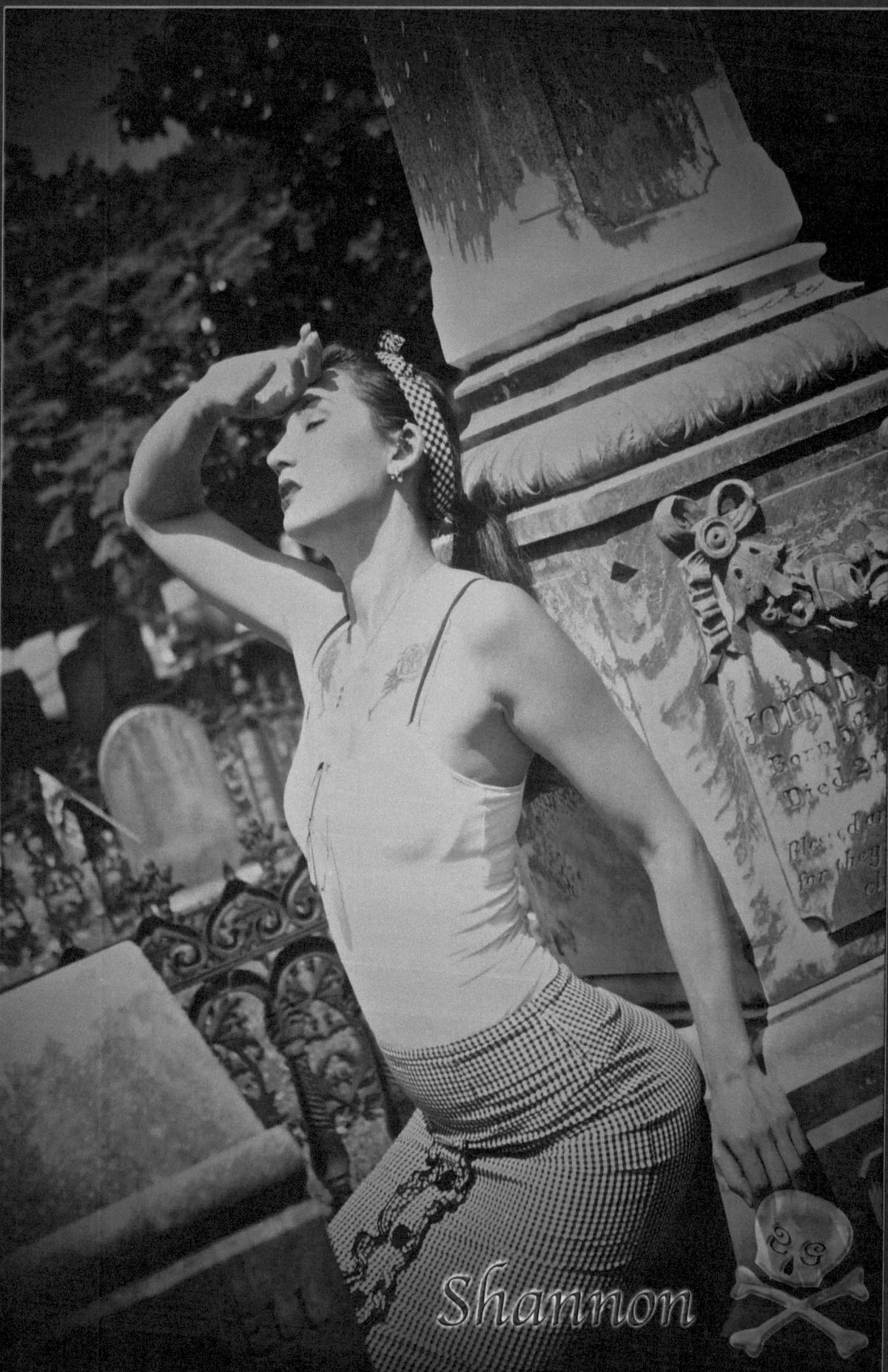

Shannon

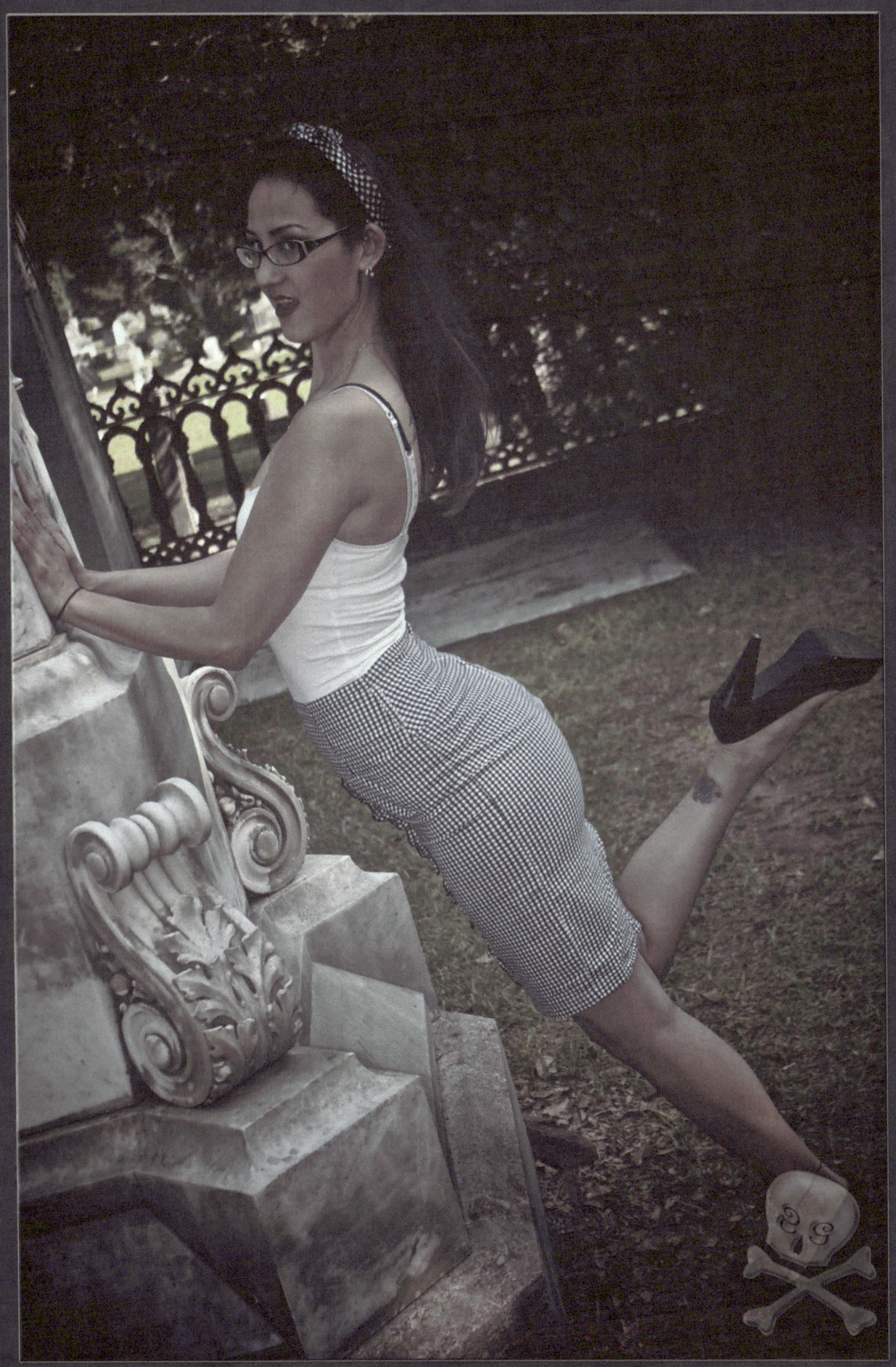

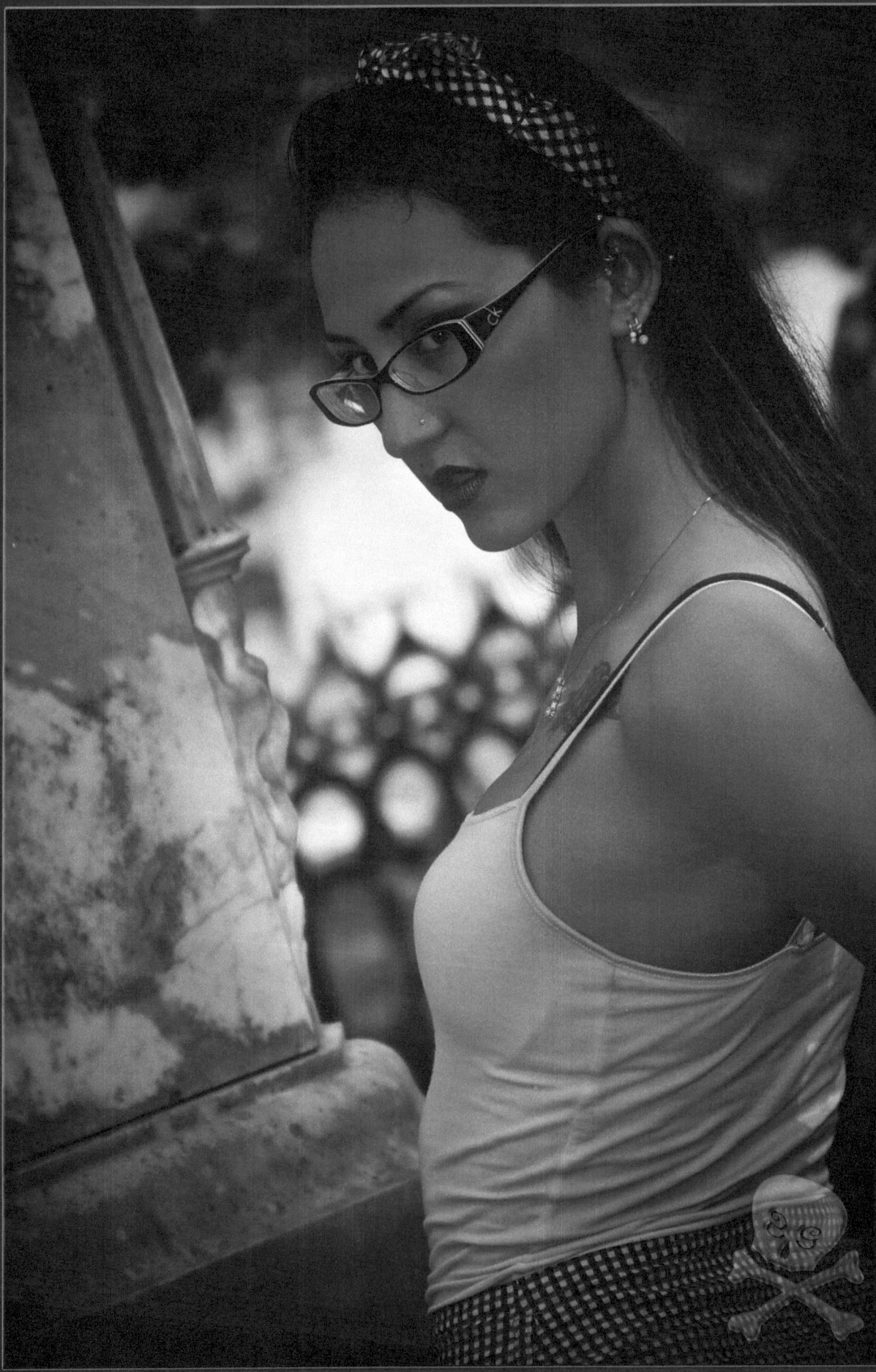

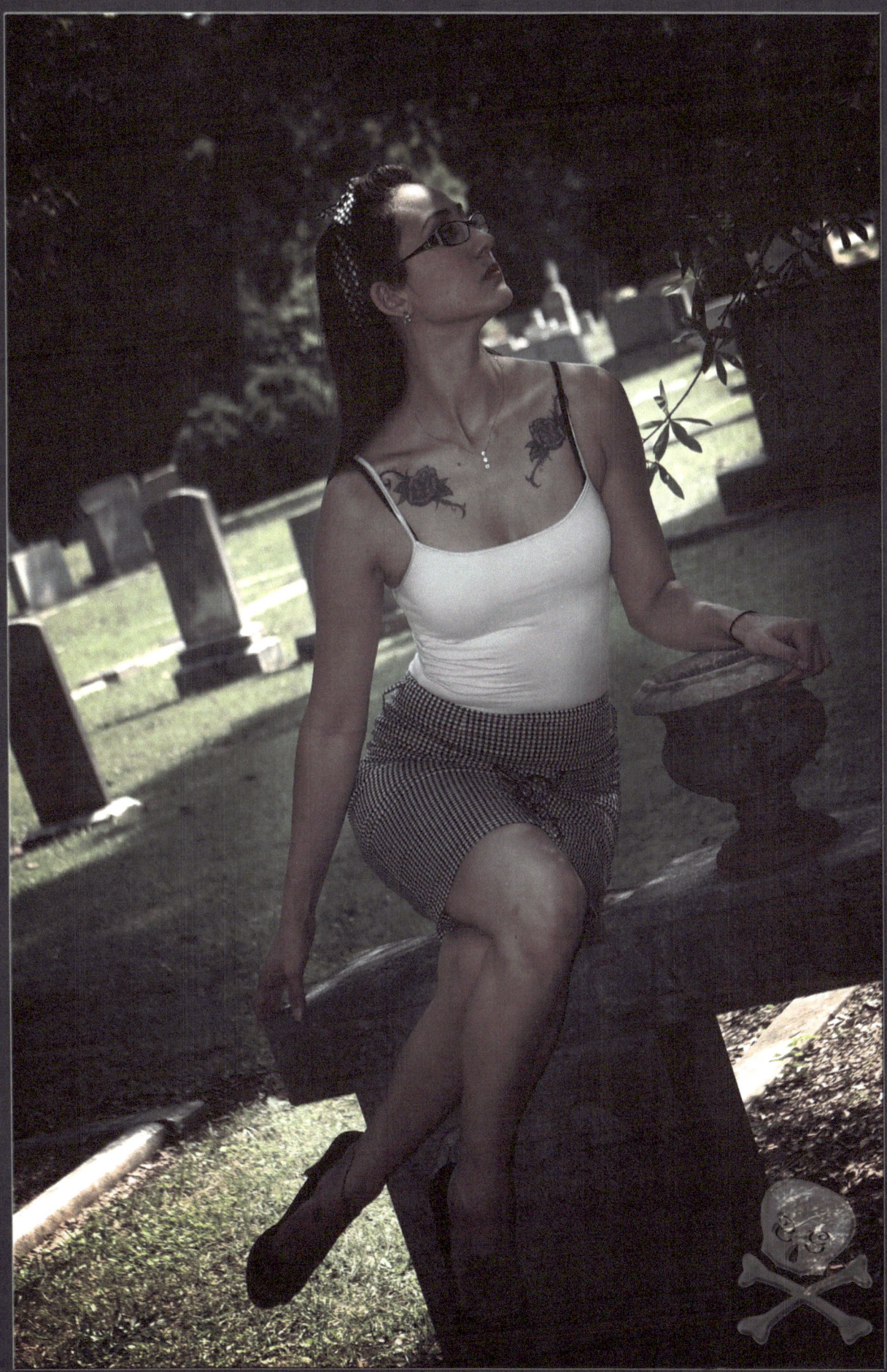

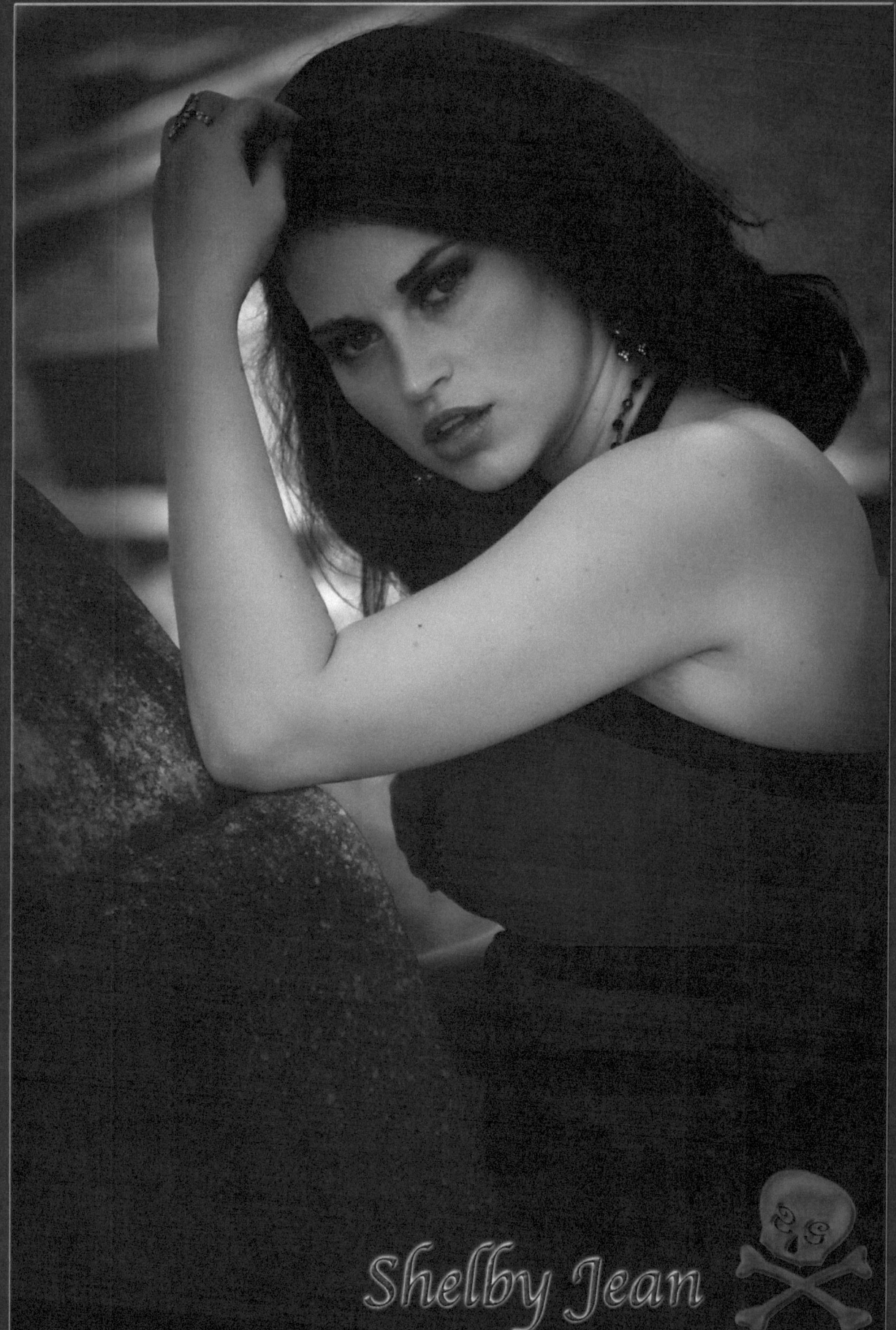

Shelby Jean

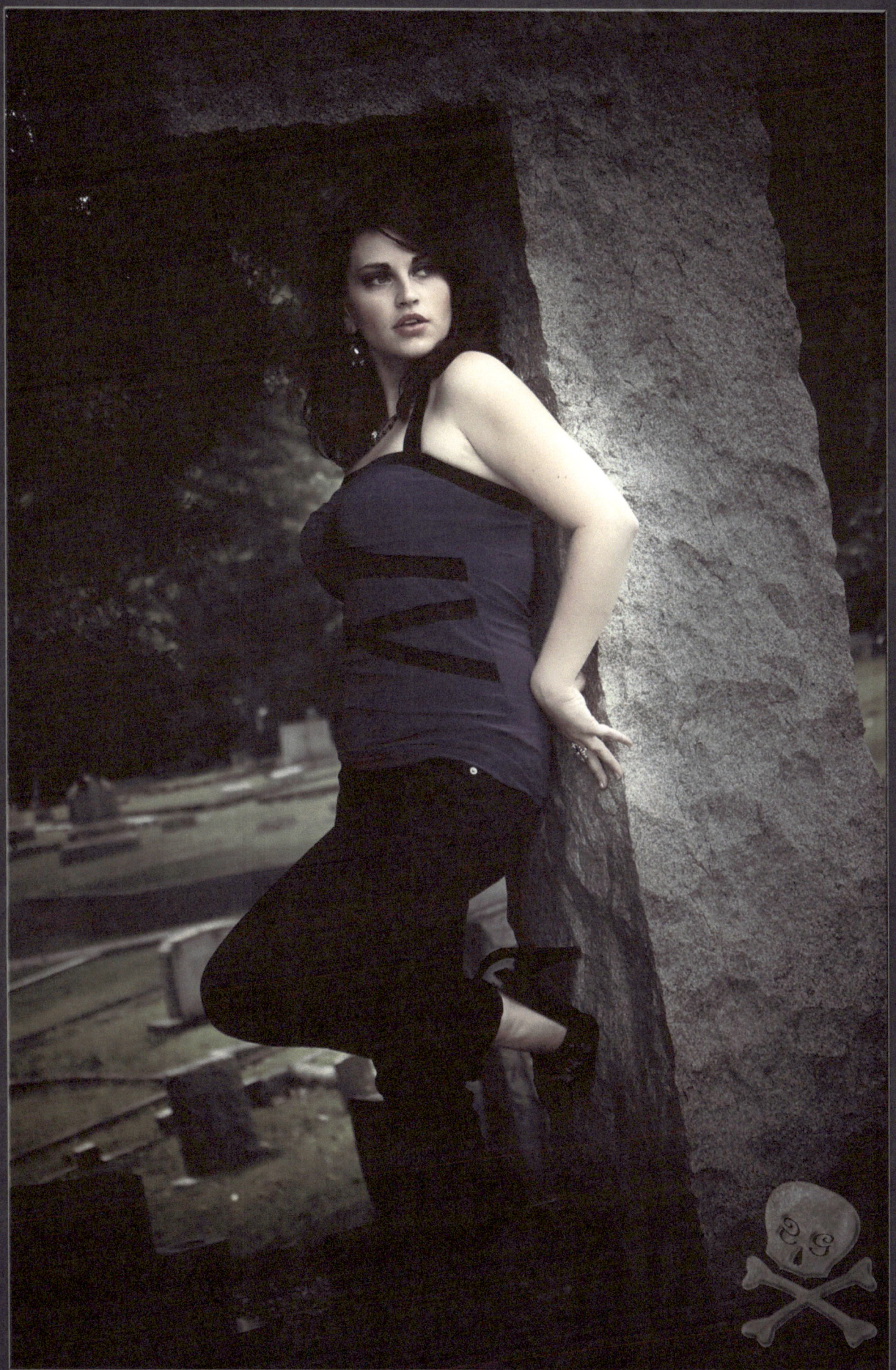

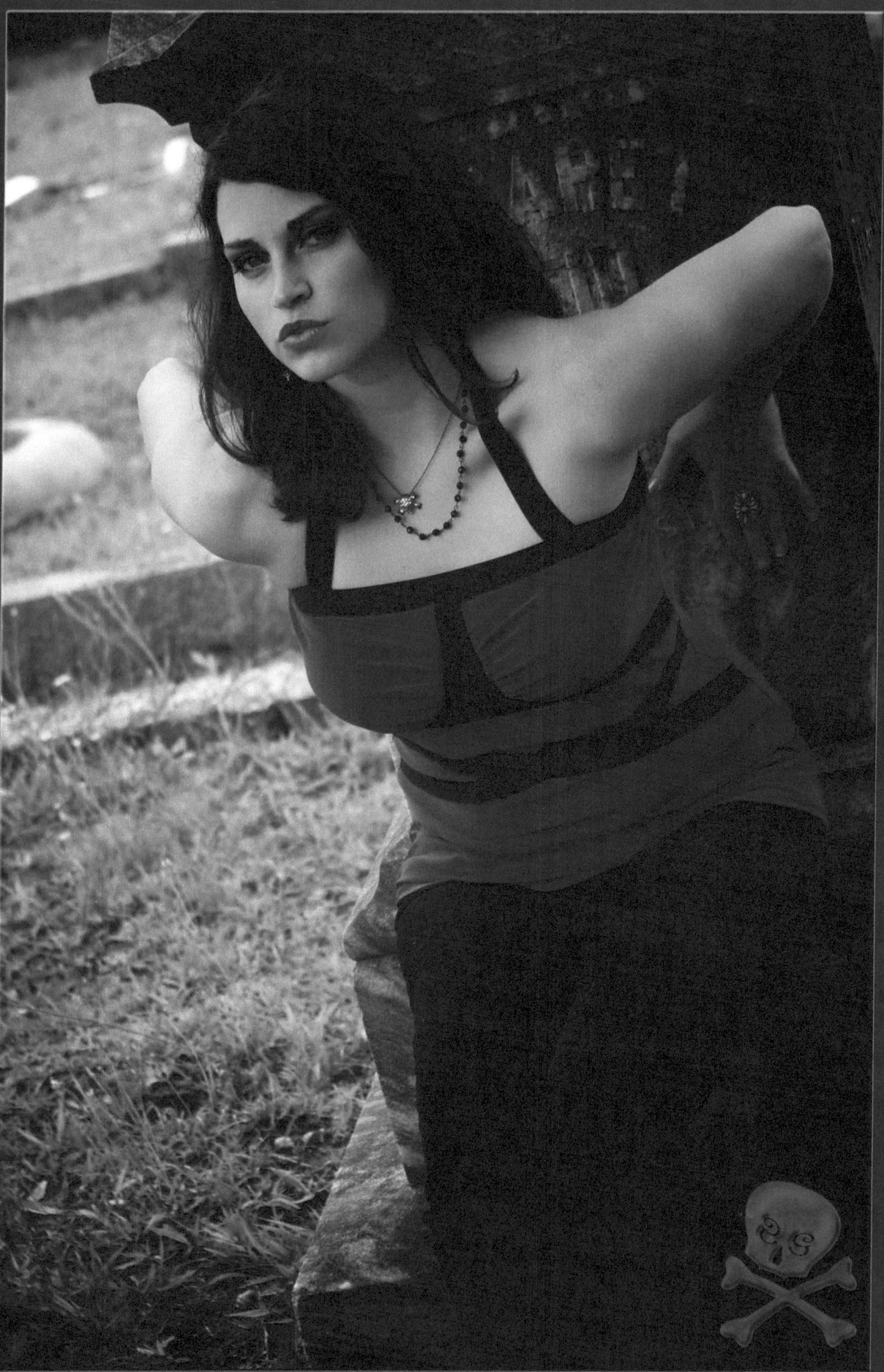

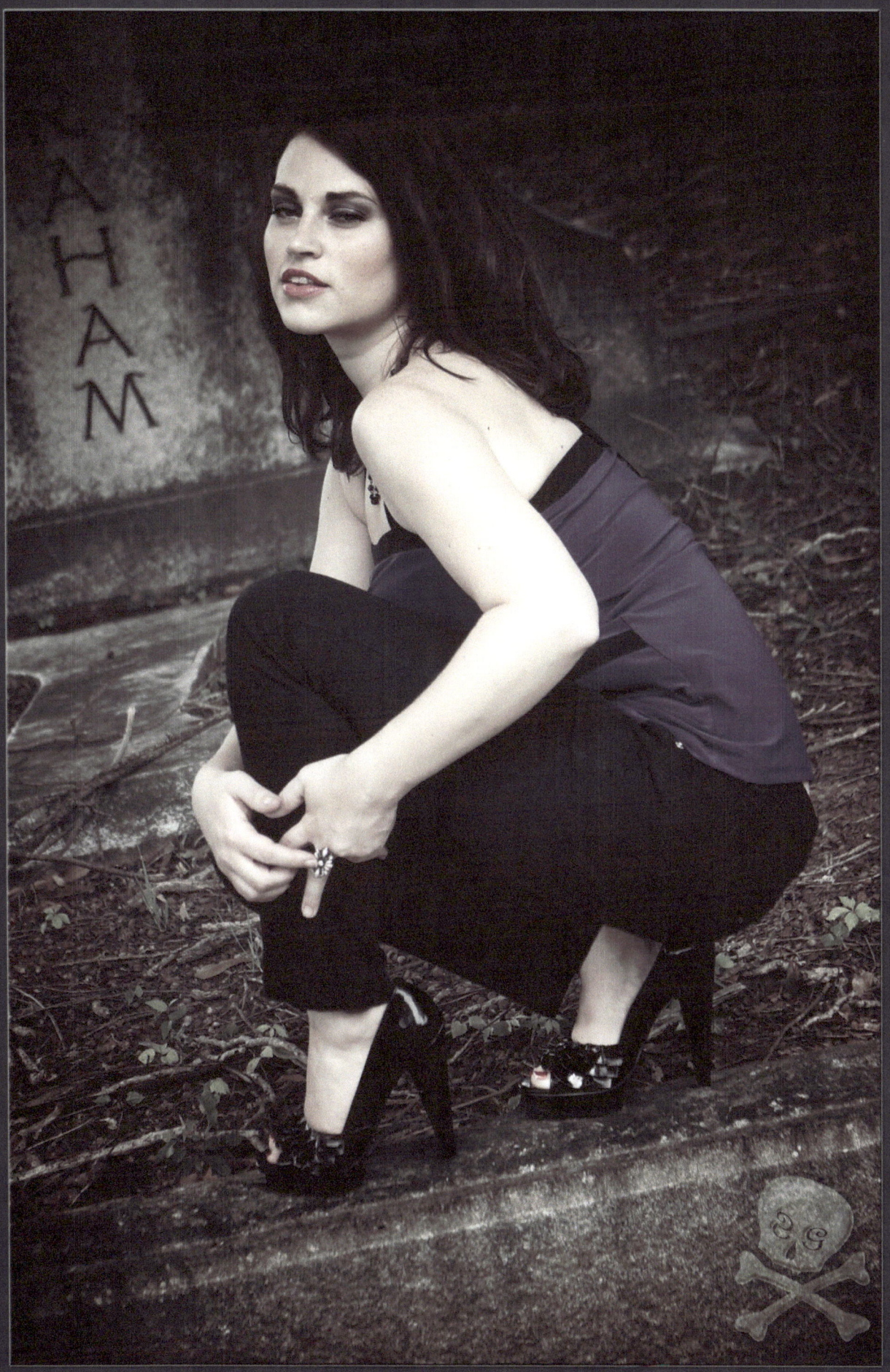

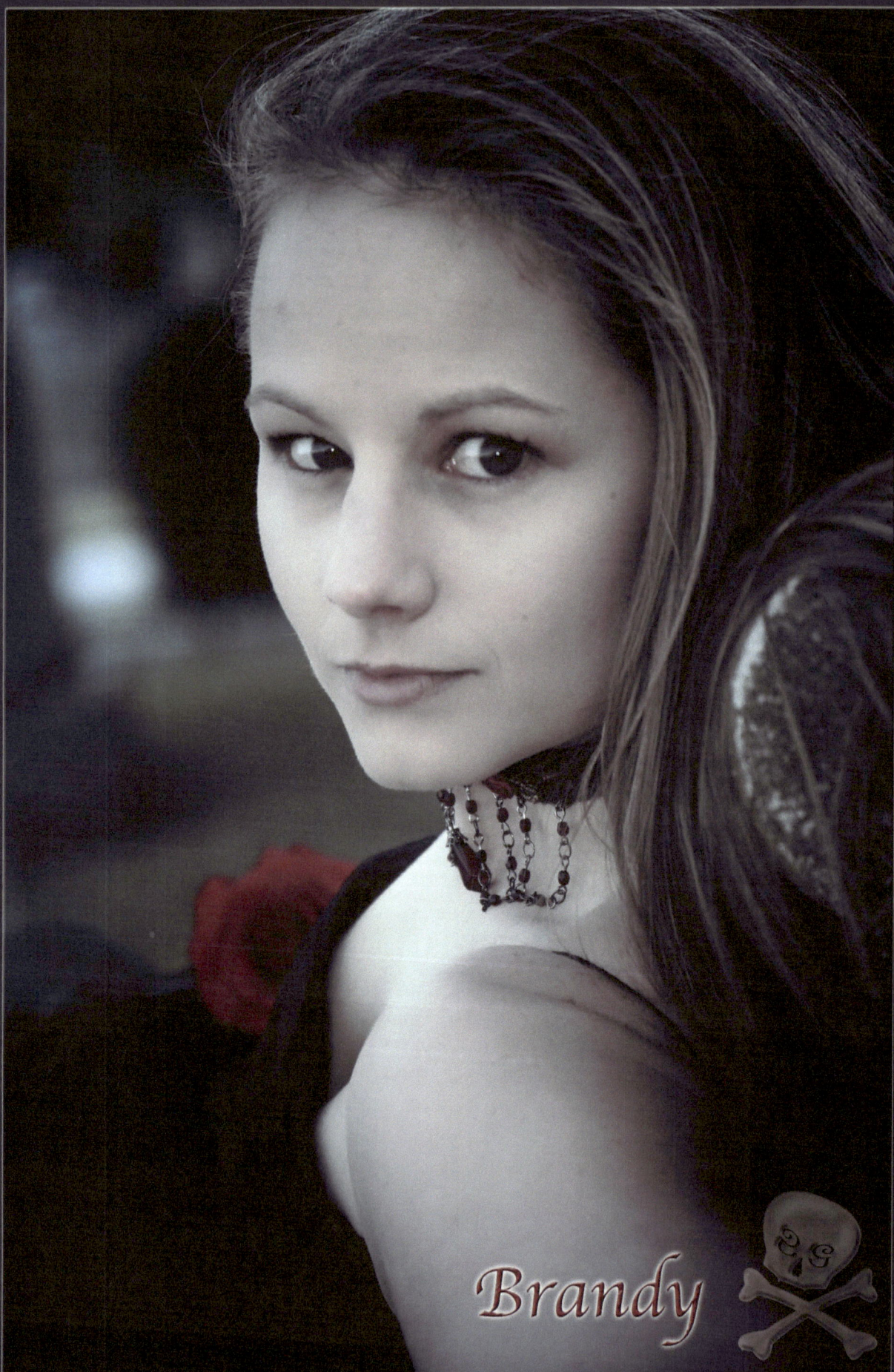

Brandy

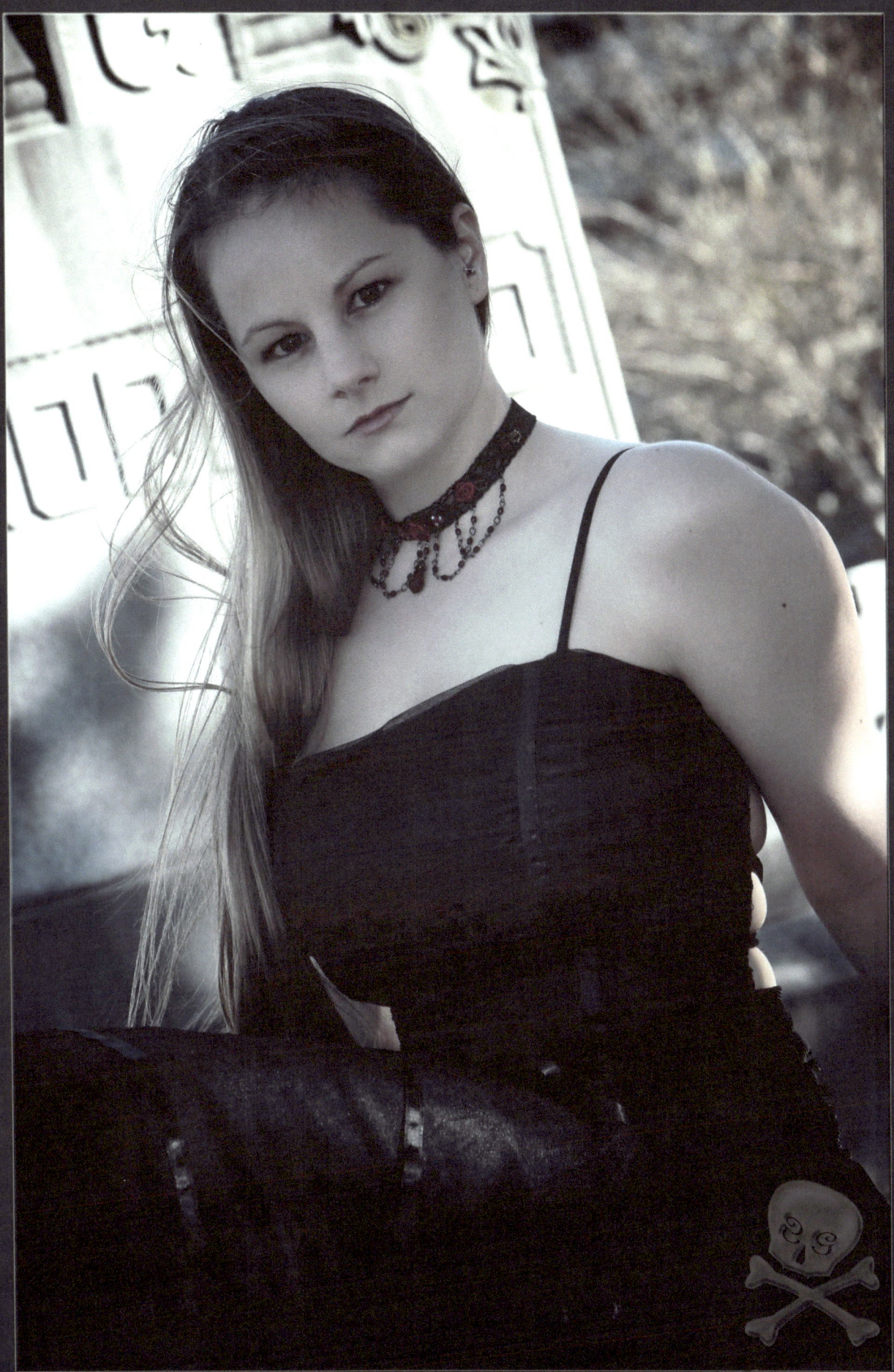

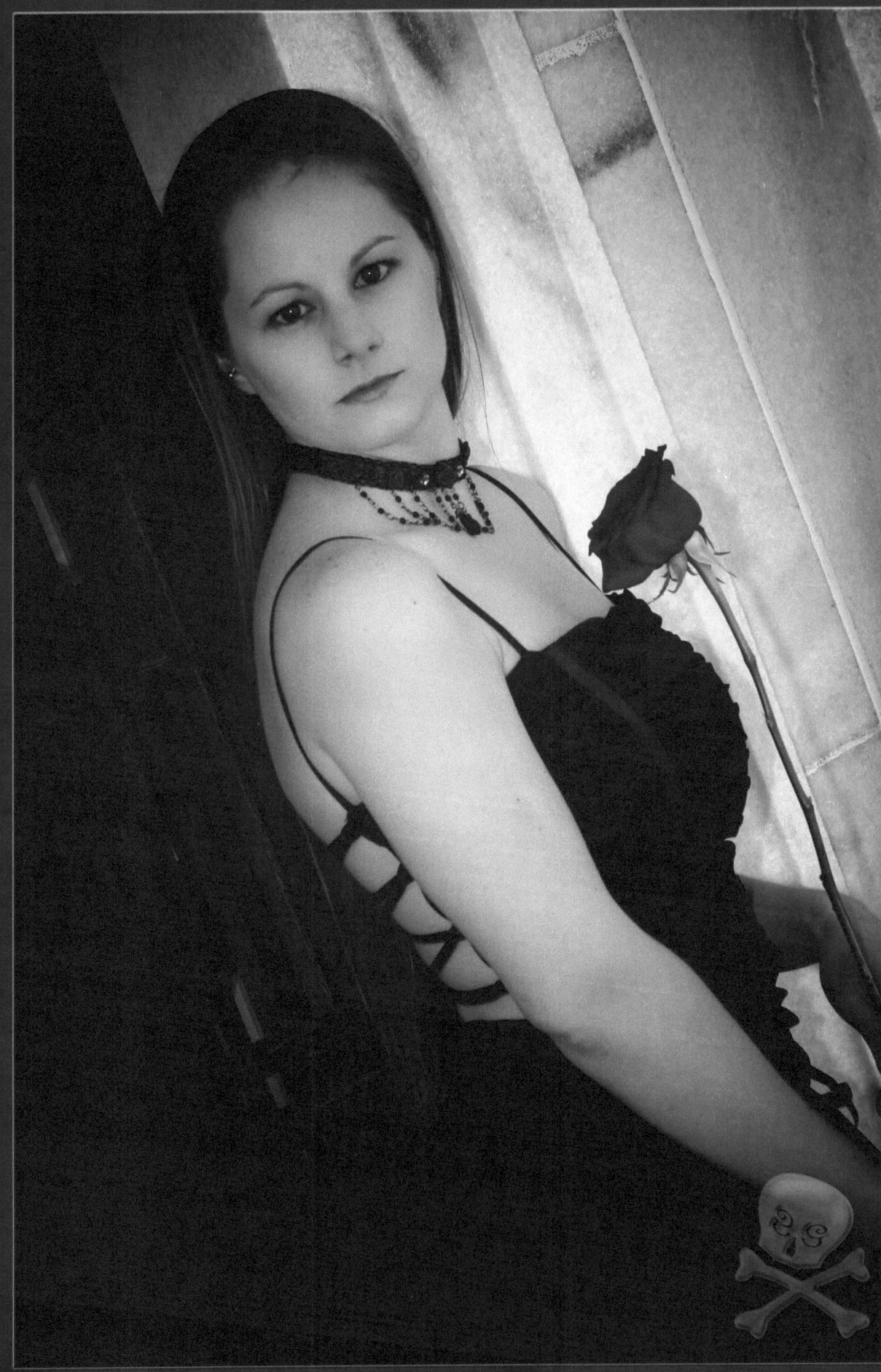

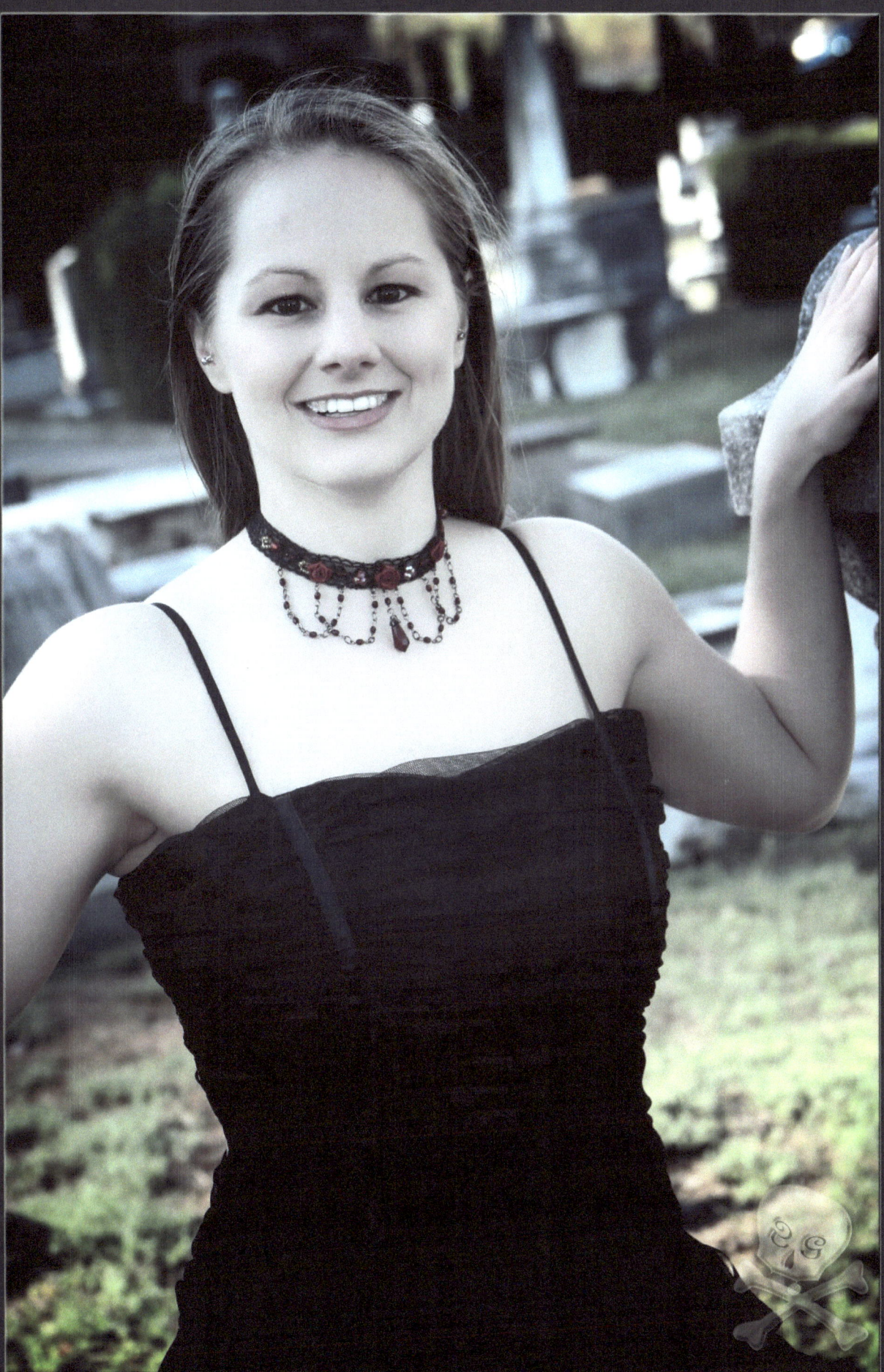

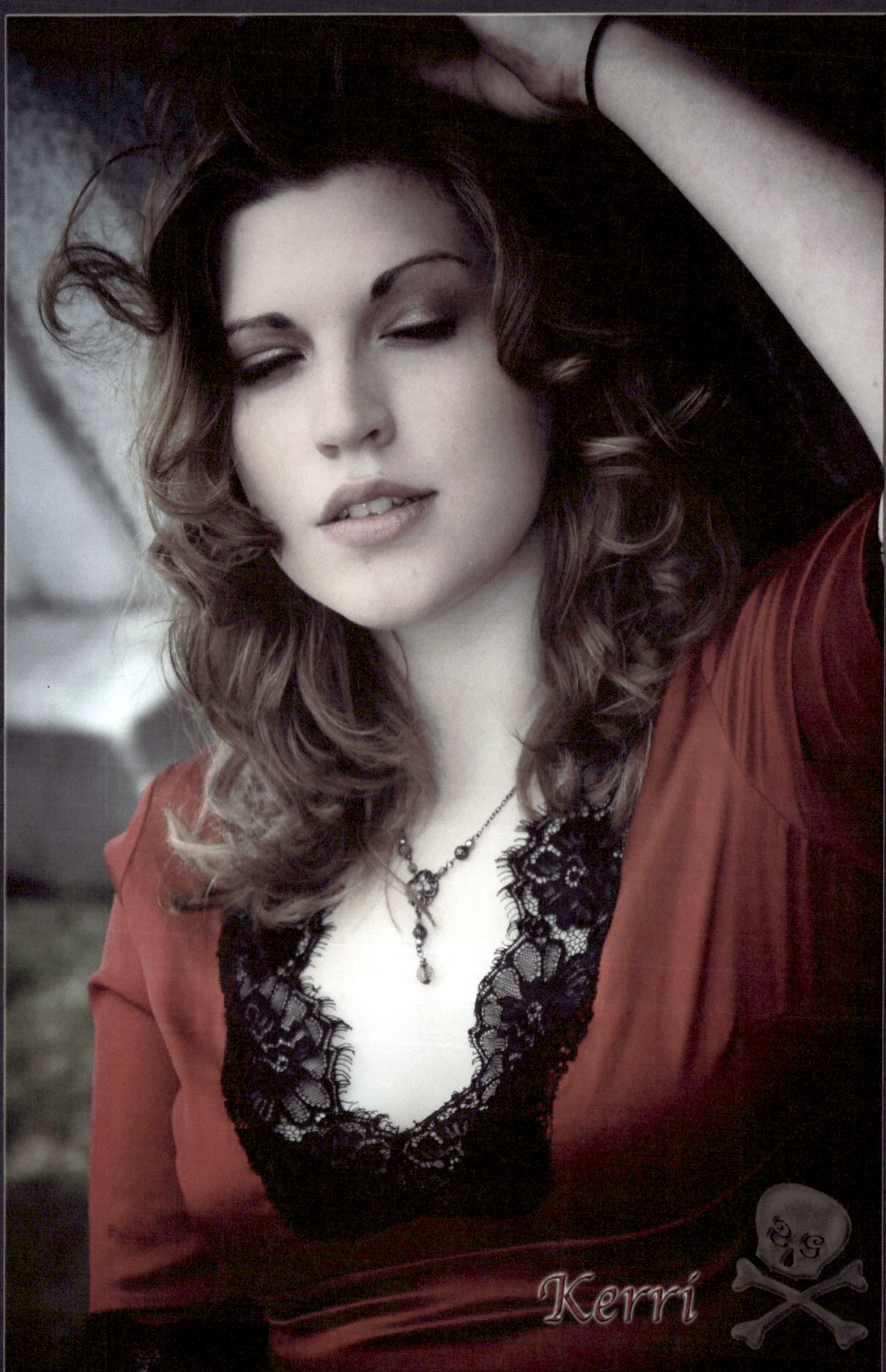

Kerri

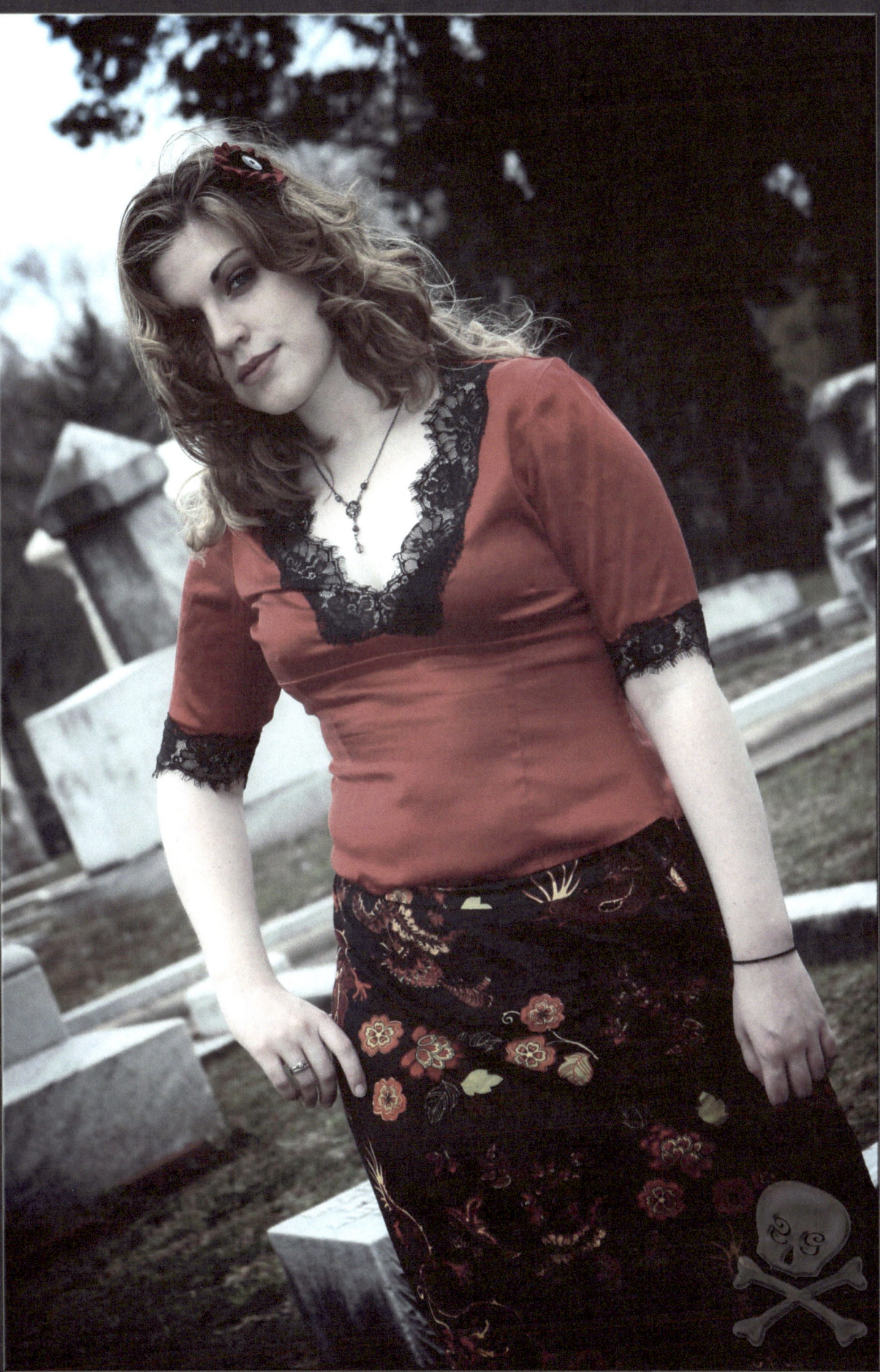

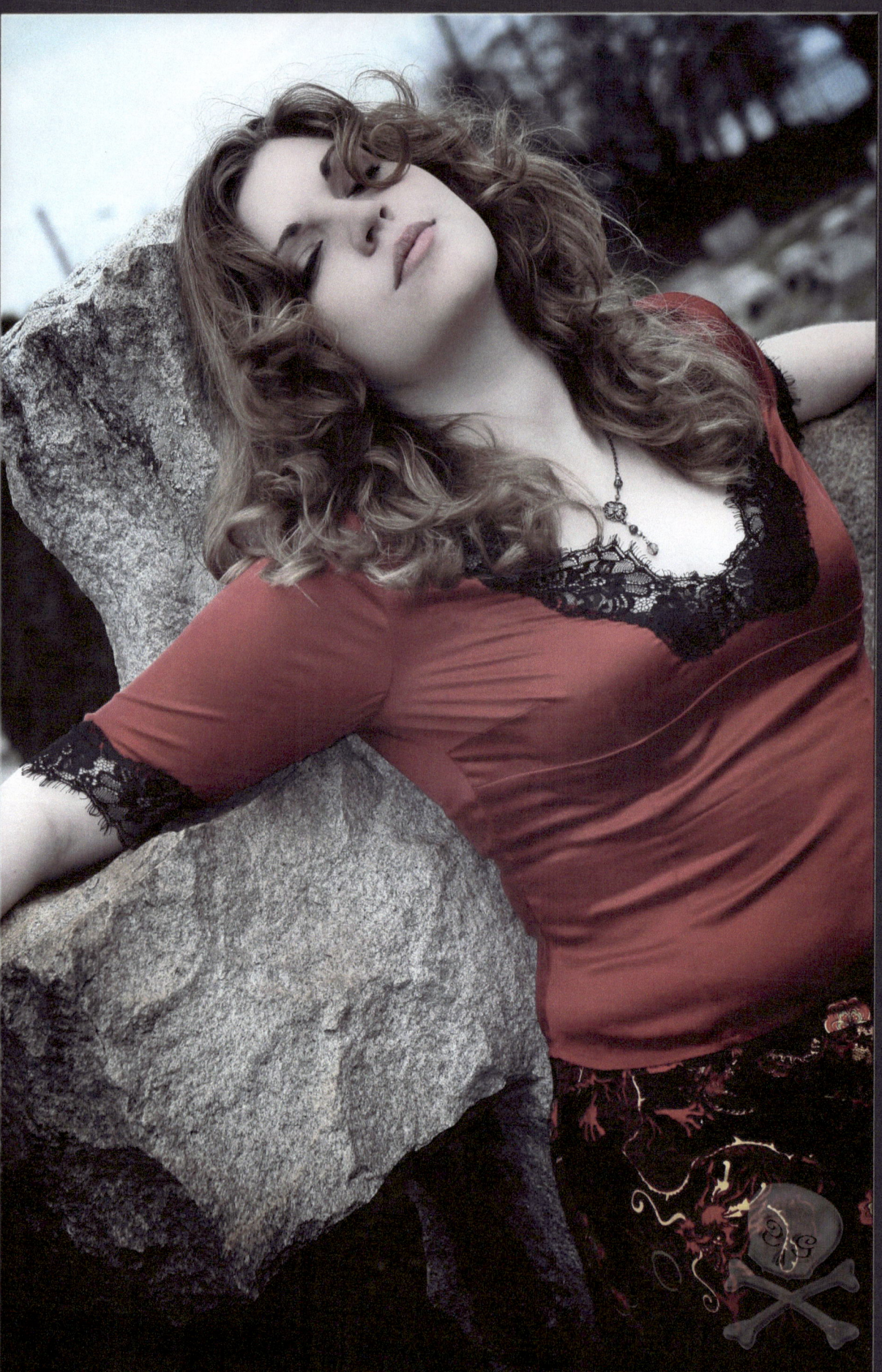

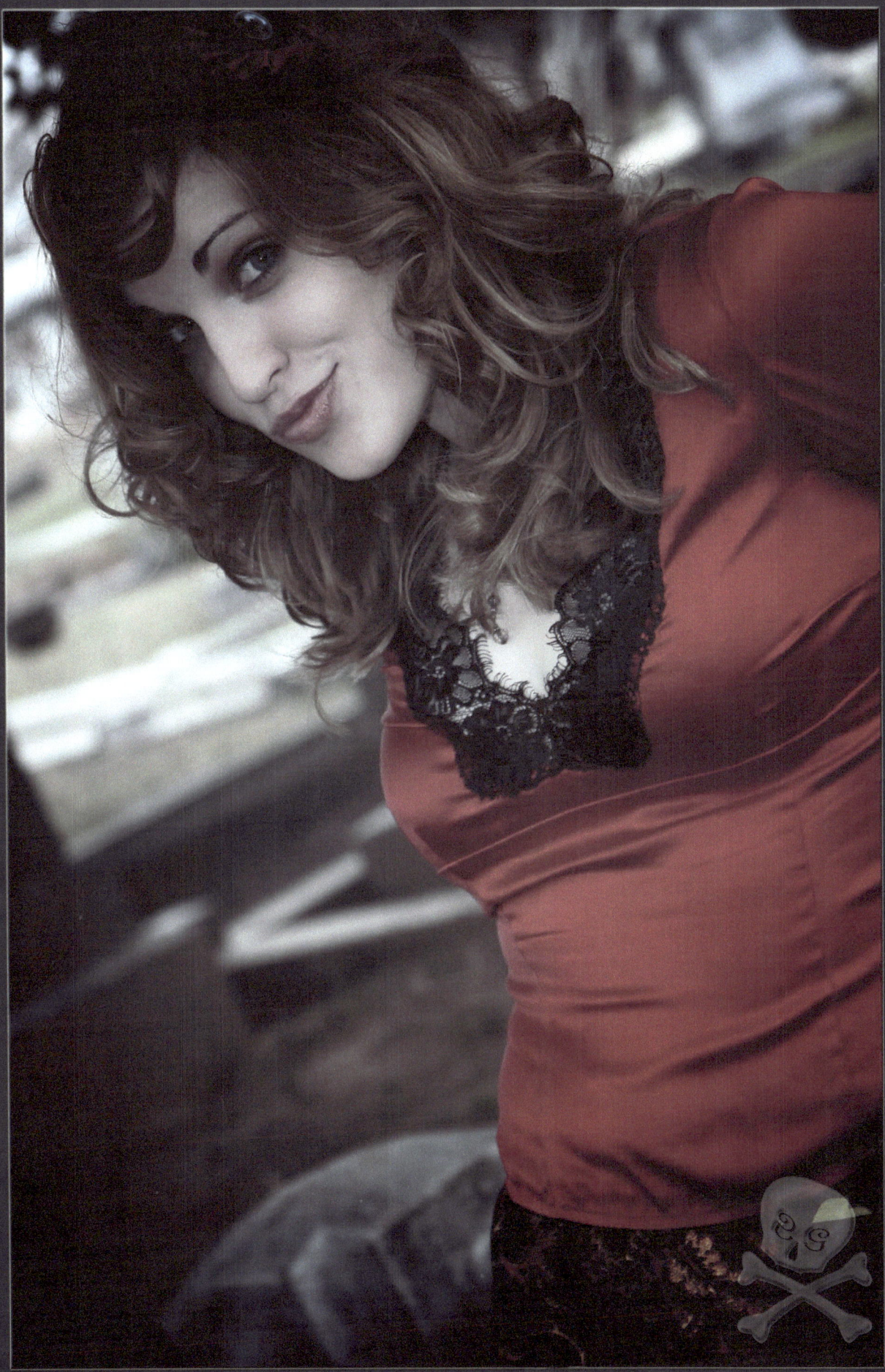

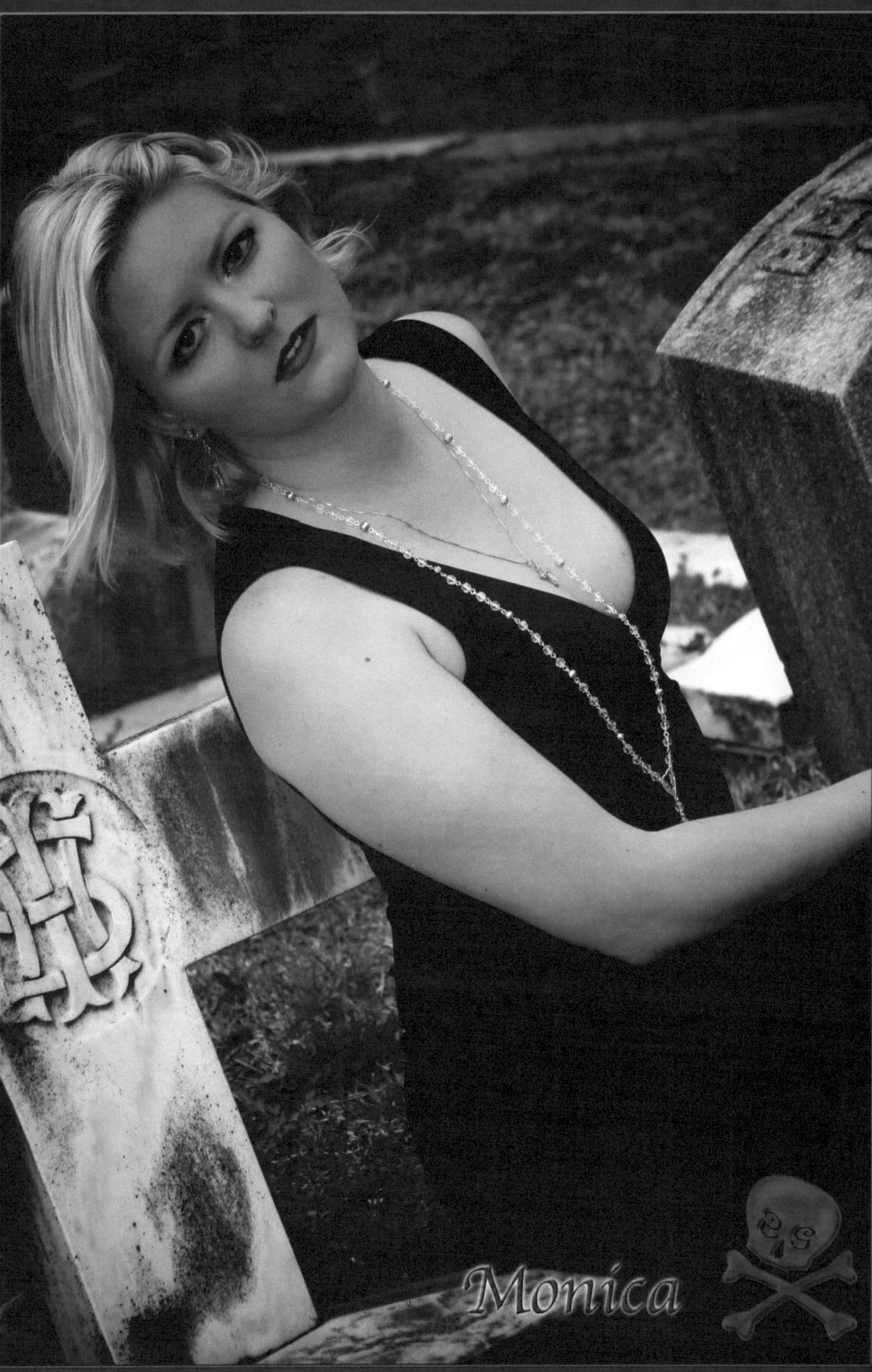

Monica

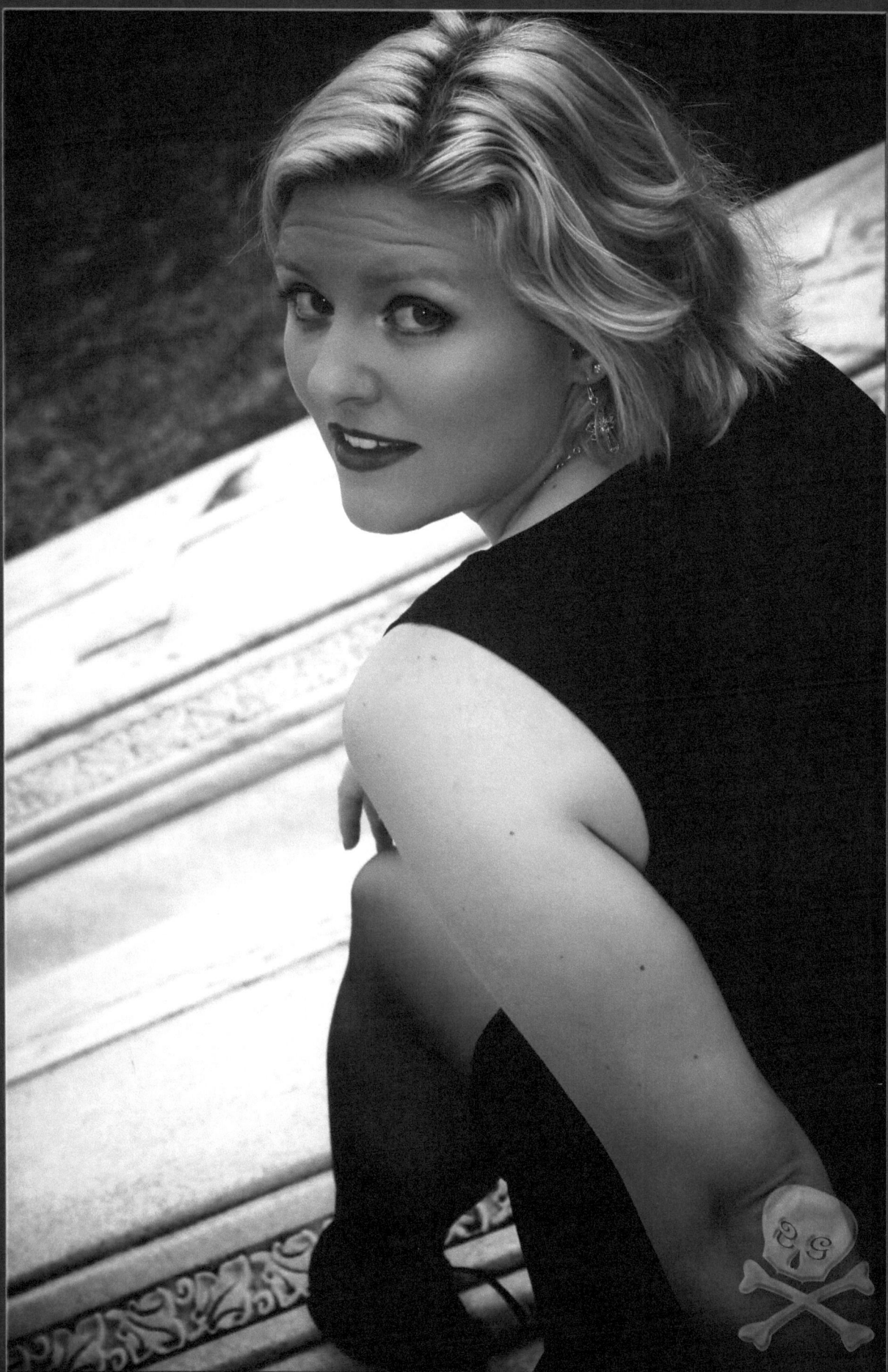

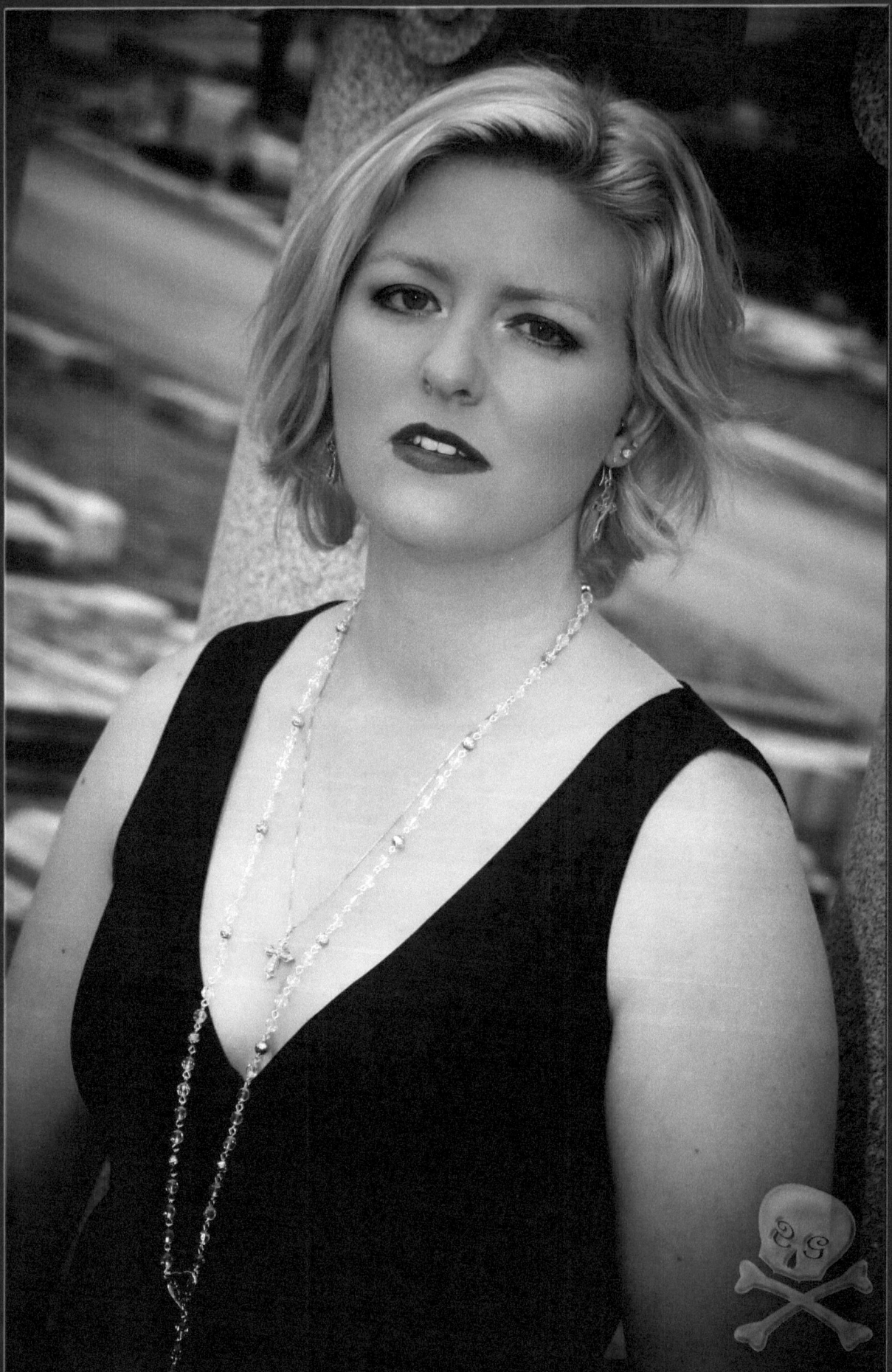

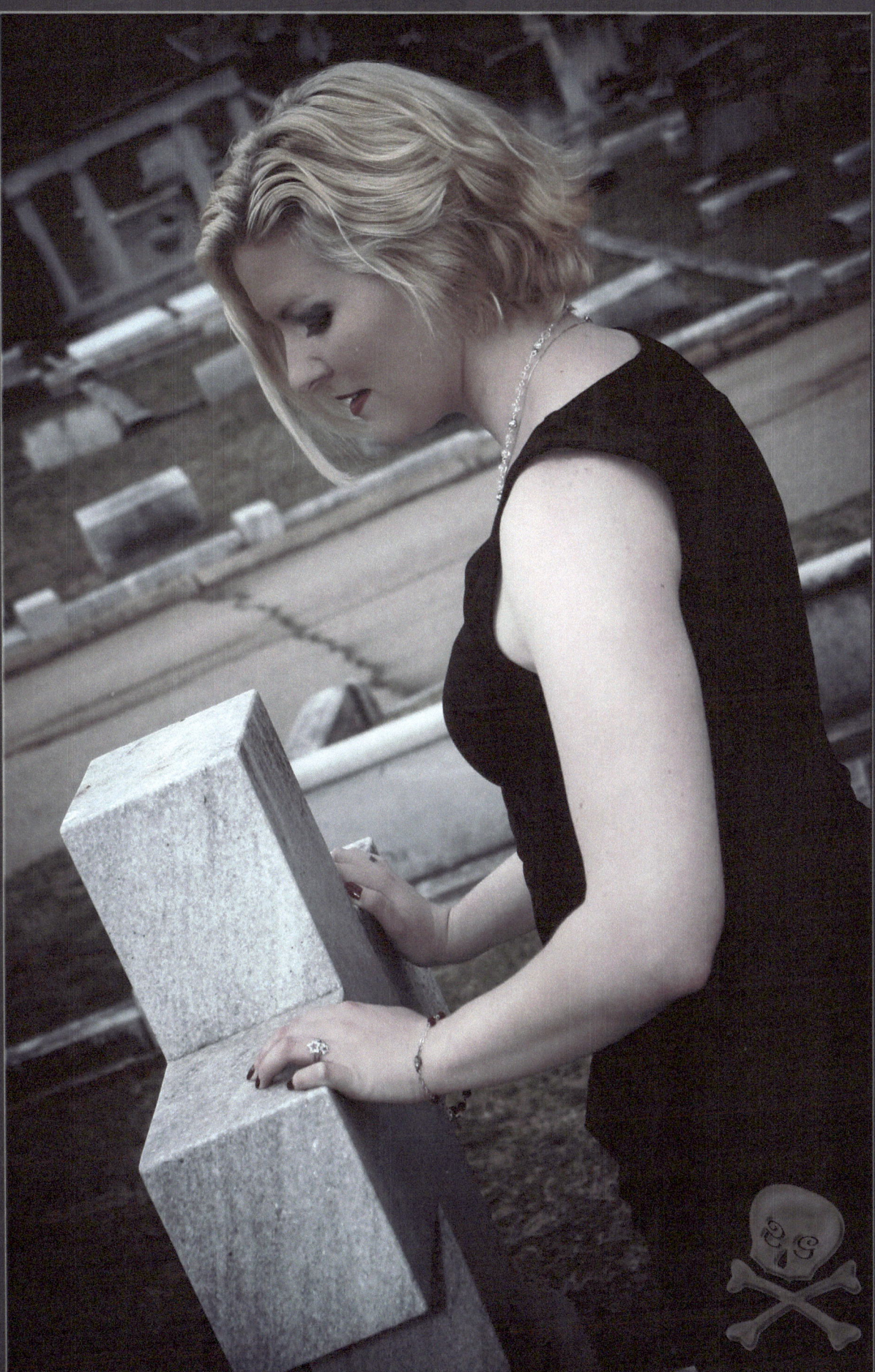

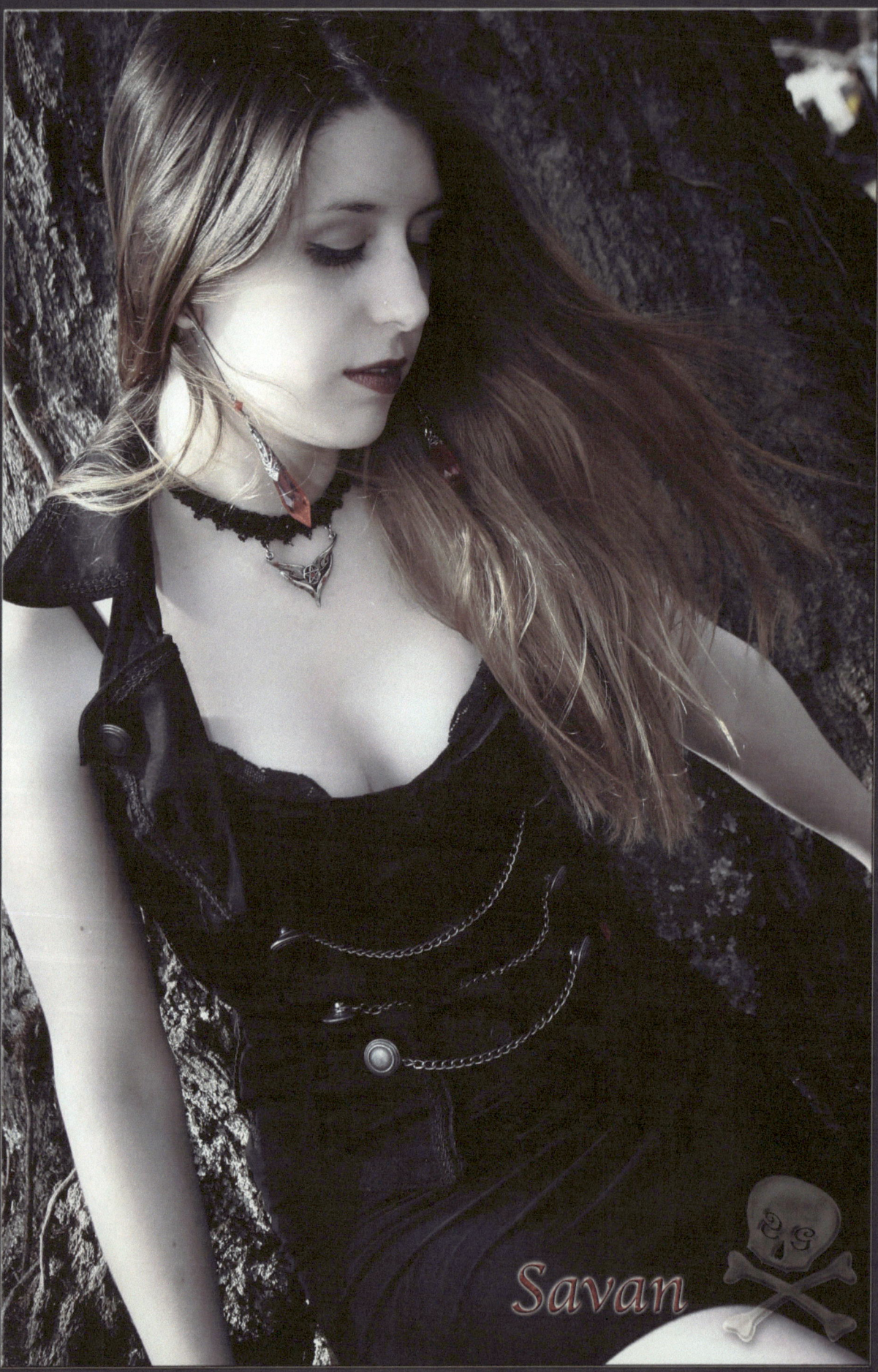

Savan

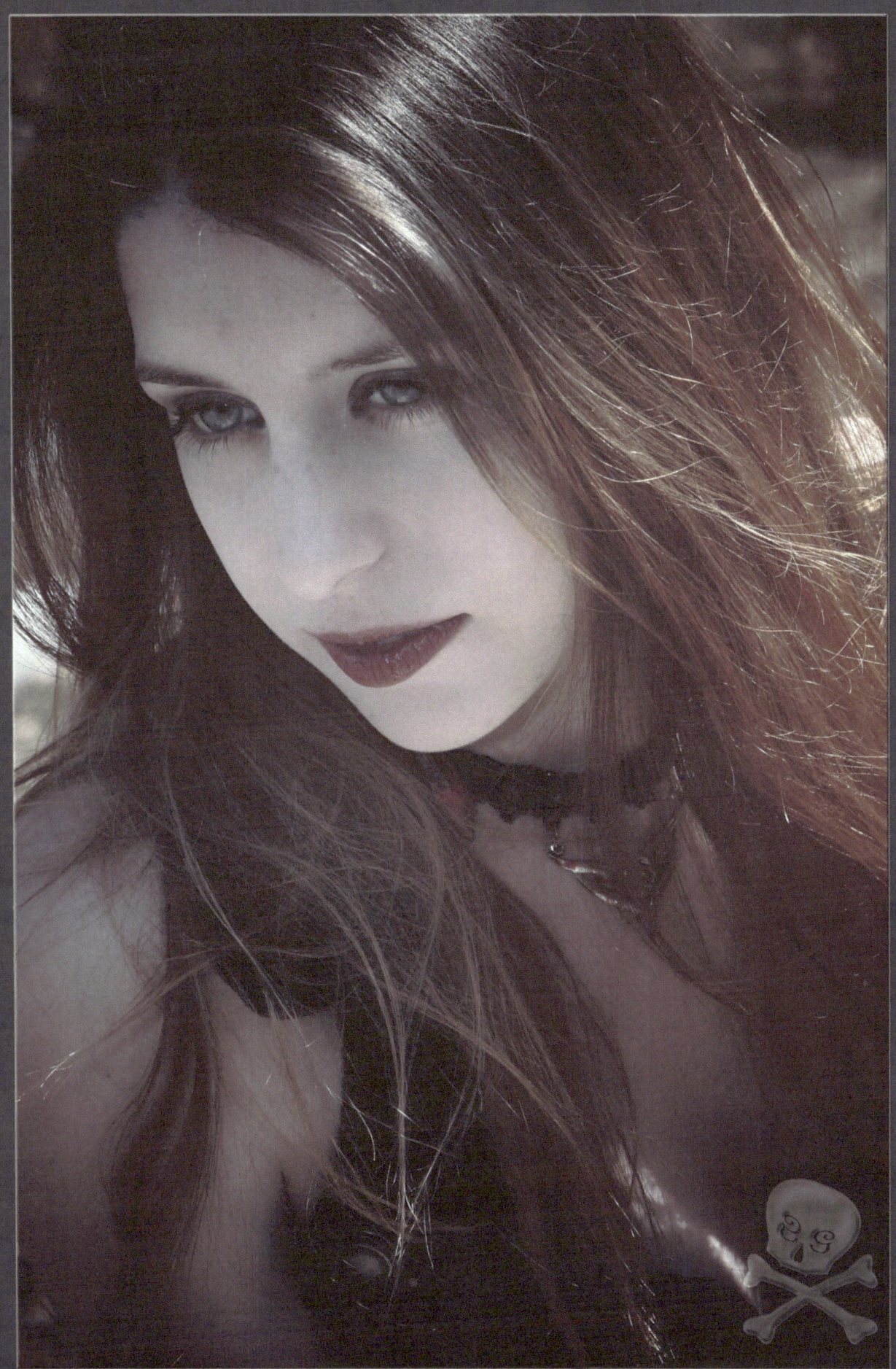

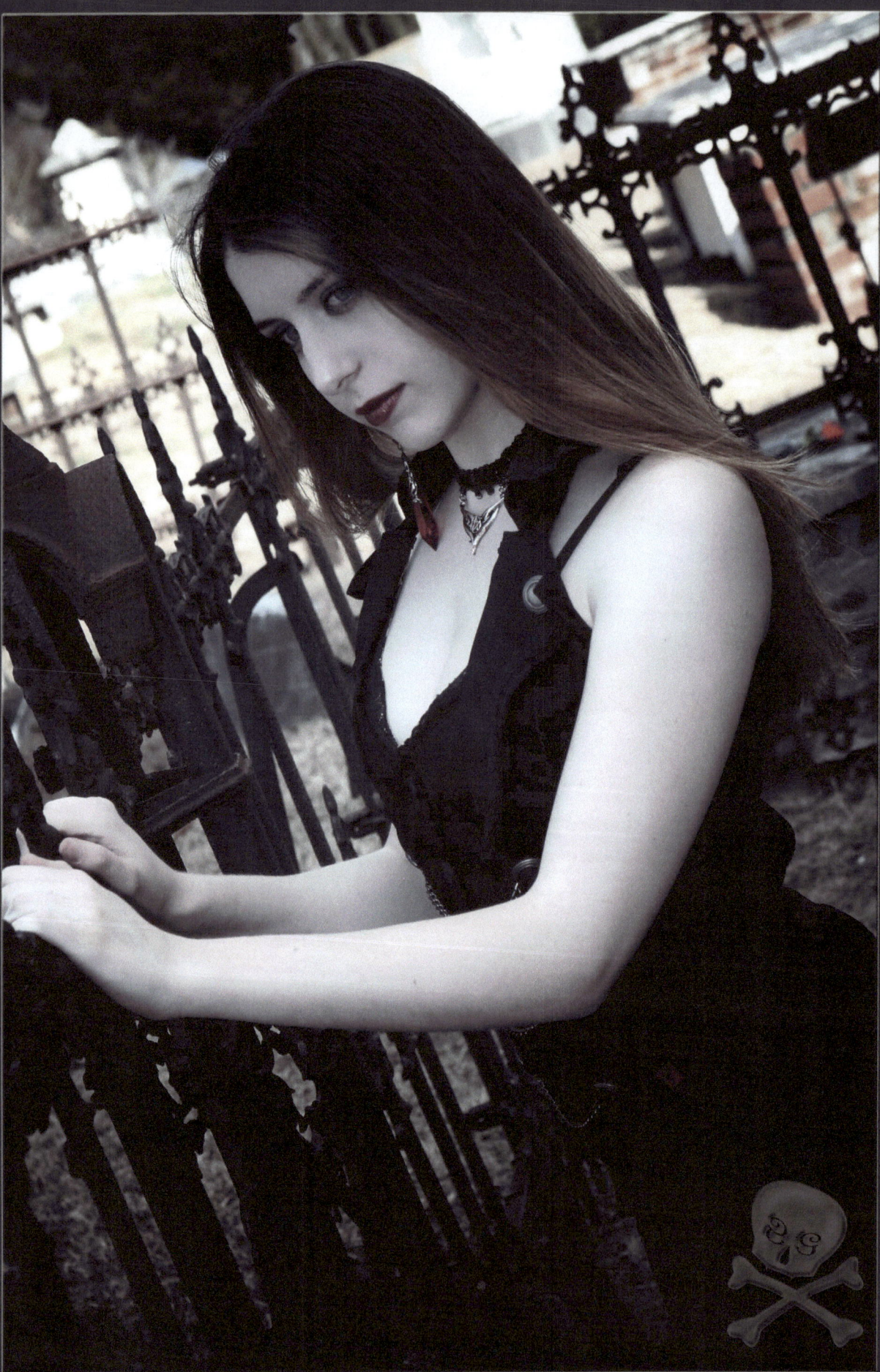

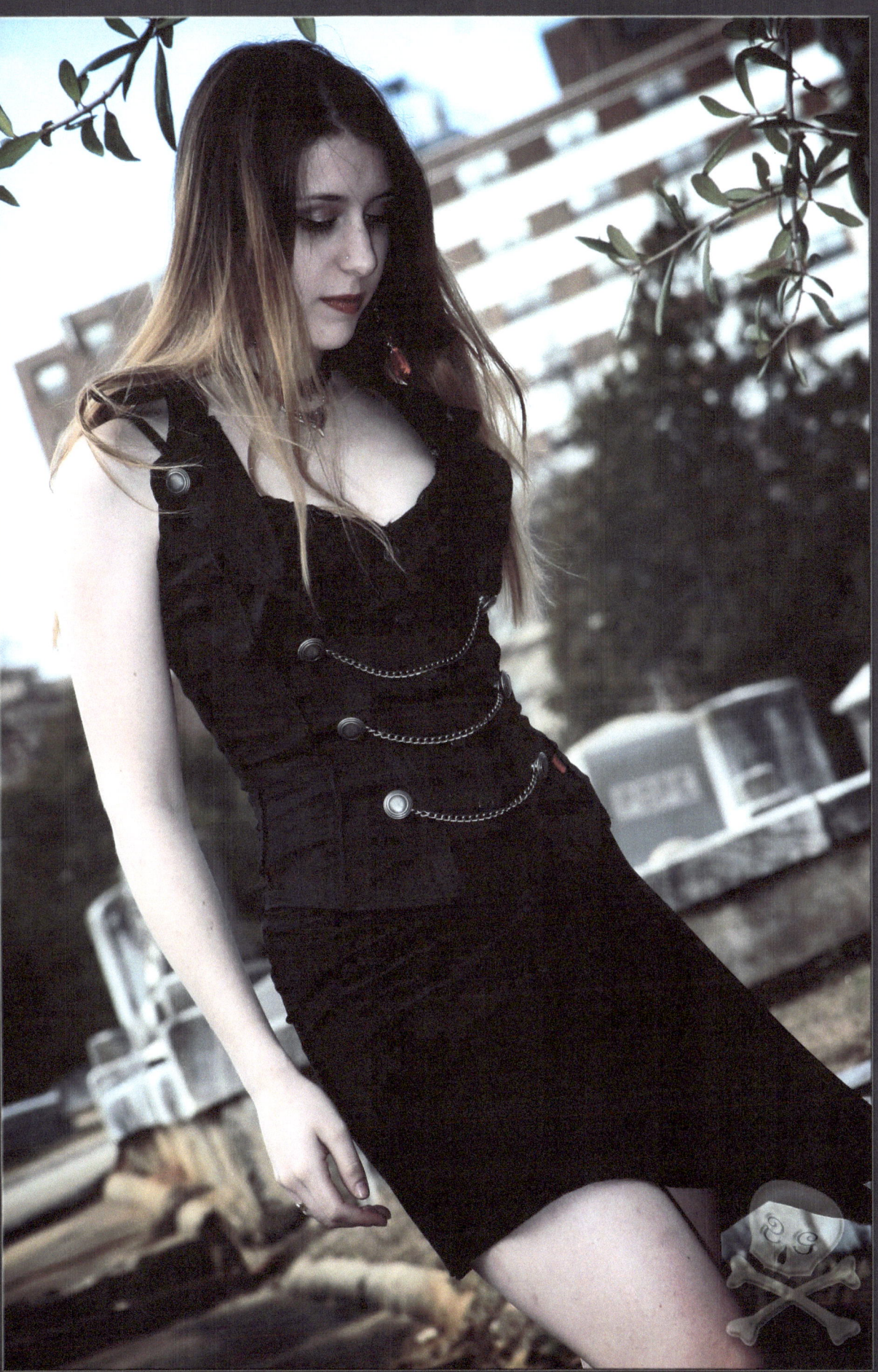

Special thanks to:

Jordan Sin, Nicci Vicious, Mina Mori, David Ward, Ehren with pervolution.com, Damon and Erin Zeiler, Dave Harlequin, Amber Teachey, Mark Carter, Angel Hjarding, and Rockin' Bones for all of the support over at Kickstarter for backing this project. All of the advance promotion has been a huge help with this book.

In addition, thanks to Earth Angel of Charlotte, NC as well as Dead Ed's of Salisbury, NC for the wardrobe contributions, and to Rockin' Bones and Folter Clothing for the incredible styling.

To my own crew from Stiff Magazine... Dave Harlequin, John "Mystic" Jennings, Justin Kates, Amara Von Nacht, David Ward, Hollie Quinn, Billy Liner, James Nimmons, and all of our contributing writers... THANK YOU ALL for standing behind what I do time and time again.

Thank you to Chris "Captain Stab Tuggo" Steele and Maybelle and my family with Psychotic Body Suspensions for giving me the opportunity to quite literally bleed for my dreams. You all have supported me without question in all of my endeavors for years, and it is not to be forgotten.

Thanks to Mick Minchow and the never ending memory of Jim Minchow, and all of my brothers and sisters at Ground Zero for giving my work a home, and to all of the bands that have worked with me over the years.

Finally, I would like to thank my friends and family for putting up with me through all of these years, especially my mother and my grandmother for looking past the overall creepyness of who I am and what I do.

www.graveyardgirls.net

www.ingramcontent.com/pod-product-compliance
Lightning Source LLC
Chambersburg PA
CBHW040742200526
45159CB00023B/1591